I0213194

Austin's

FLOWER HILL

LEGACY

Austin's FLOWER HILL LEGACY

A Remarkable Family & a Sixth Street Wildscape

ROSA WALSTON LATIMER

Foreword by Robin Grace Soto

THE
History
PRESS

Published by The History Press
Charleston, SC
www.historypress.com

Copyright © 2021 by Rosa Walston Latimer
All rights reserved

First published 2021

ISBN 9781467149396

Library of Congress Control Number: 2021943813

Notice: The information in this book is true and complete to the best of our knowledge. It is offered without guarantee on the part of the author or The History Press. The author and The History Press disclaim all liability in connection with the use of this book.

All rights reserved. No part of this book may be reproduced or transmitted in any form whatsoever without prior written permission from the publisher except in the case of brief quotations embodied in critical articles and reviews.

Dedicated to
John Plyler

The consummate caretaker of Flower Hill
and trustee of Miss Jane Smoot's vision for preserving the
Smoot family legacy.

CONTENTS

Foreword

LETTERS, DIARIES, ALBUMS AND SPOONS

*E*verything all at once. That is what it feels like to walk onto the dining porch at Flower Hill, surrounded by planks of petrified wood and geodes the size of beach balls. Or to stand at the top of the horse collar drive in a field of fool's onions, redbuds and spiderworts. To open a hidden drawer on a roll-top desk and exhume a sentimental collection of coins, a package of postcards sent home from World War II, a ticket stub from a matinée showing of *The Love Parade*. Daily I find myself in conversation and collaboration with the past, present and future, all at once. In the spring of 2016, I joined Flower Hill as the director of what would become the Flower Hill Urban Homestead Museum. The very first conversation I had with the home took place on the north sleeping porch, surrounded by towers of caned-back chairs, rows of ancient metal filing cabinets and an assortment of wooden wardrobes. I introduced myself. Asked where I should begin. Already feeling the sensation of everything all at once. My eyes landed on a file drawer labeled in loping cursive: *Letters, Diaries, Albums, and Spoons*. One of hundreds of labels left behind by Miss Jane Smoot, a teacher, traveler, citizen historian and Flower Hill's last inhabitant.

The greatest lesson I have learned since that first conversation, after opening that drawer and countless others, is what it truly means to be a home.

For more than 140 years, Flower Hill has been home to all sorts of families. It has held mothers and their babies. It has watched children return from bad days at school and young teachers head out to lead their first day of instruction. It has watched soldiers return from war. The

Spanish American War, World War I, World War II, Korea, Vietnam. It sheltered the Smoot family through the 1918 influenza pandemic. It provided a refuge for me, the board, volunteers and our community during the coronavirus pandemic of 2020.

It has patiently listened to gramophones, radio programs and television sets as Dr. King shared a dream, man walked on the moon, the Beatles invaded America and Mr. Rogers welcomed us to the neighborhood.

This home has felt the bounty of plenty and the agony of scarcity, and for a very short period of time, which I imagine was the hardest time, it stood empty—it felt alone—without family. Then, one by one, new community members arrived and began to call it home again. Historians, preservationists, painters, filmmakers, students, teachers, travelers, ecologists, woodworkers and writers. In 2019, during a Saturday morning tour, Flower Hill welcomed author and historian Rosa Latimer.

During the 130 years that the Smoot family lived at Flower Hill, they played host to countless relatives, university students and traveling artists. In exchange for room and board, these artists would leave behind a painting, ceramic vase or etching. A piece of themselves inspired by the conversation and collaboration they experienced at Flower Hill. Rosa joined the Flower Hill's Artist-in-Residence program in 2020, embracing the opportunity to honor and explore the artists who had come before her and the home that had welcomed and inspired them. This book is perhaps the greatest gift left behind. For it holds all of the conversations and contributions that came before her. Rosa's tireless research, personal voice and sweeping vision have found a way to hold and share everything Flower Hill was, is or will be—all at once. In John Hejduk's poem "Sentences on a House," the speaker tells us, "[A] house knows who loves it." Rosa, I hope you know that Flower Hill loves you, too.

At the very back of the *Letters, Diaries, Albums, and Spoons* file drawer, I discovered a shoebox filled with cassette tapes. Twenty-six hours of Miss Jane Smoot's oral history. In one of the later tapings, in between an exploration of her teaching philosophy and detailed stories of her childhood growing up in the young city of Austin, Miss Smoot reminds us that people living through time are intrinsic treasures. Everyone has a story to tell. Everyone is worth a book.

Robin Grace Soto
Founding and Executive Director
Flower Hill Urban Homestead Museum

ACKNOWLEDGMENTS

While I may have written the final words of this book, you'll see the work of Robin Grace Soto throughout. As executive director, she has overseen the preservation of all things Flower Hill and has done so with a caring, loving heart.

Volunteers Melissa Keane and Felicia Kongable invested many hours organizing and cataloguing the Flower Hill archives long before I entered the picture. That work and their many contributions while I worked on this book make them an essential part of this project.

Thank you, Laura Velez, for telling me about this beautiful, historic property and encouraging me to take a tour.

Special thanks to Mica McCook, Austin photographer, for the spectacular cover photo of the fool's onions in bloom at Flower Hill.

Thank you to Ace and Sara Belknap for your support and eleventh-hour fact-checking.

For your never-wavering loving care and positive influence in my life—thank you, Lara Latimer!

INTRODUCTION

*A*s you step between the impressive columns onto the wide, shaded front porch of Flower Hill, you are inclined to look south and take in the beauty of the serene surroundings. For over 130 years, the Smoot family "cooperated with nature" to create this expansive landscape. Depending on the season, you may see an abundance of *Triteleia hyacinthina*, also known as fool's onion, in bloom. The caretaker of this expanse for over three decades, John Plyler, describes this covering of white flowers as resembling a blanket of snow. Other seasons bring lantana, red spider lilies and delicate chili lilies, amid dozens of other colorful plants. The many trees on the estate were placed intentionally over 100 years ago to take advantage of their beauty.

With an appreciation of the surroundings, you wonder how this peaceful, rural atmosphere can exist less than two hundred feet from the classic iron gate that opens onto West Sixth Street, one of the busiest streets in the city. That modern-day thoroughfare is of no concern as you allow yourself to absorb the ambiance of yesteryear.

Leaving the view of this generous Texas wildscape, you open the double black walnut doors and enter the front hall of the Smoot family home built in 1877. To the left, you can imagine Dr. Reverend Smoot sitting at his massive, cluttered desk reviewing his Sunday sermon or preparing a reading list for his theology students. A few steps farther down the hall, you instinctively brush your hand along the railing and wonder what is at the top of the stairs. However, that discovery will have to wait, as you

Above: Flower Hill, home to three generations of the Smoot family, is on the National Register of Historical Places. *Flower Hill Foundation Collection.*

Opposite, top: The Flower Hill foyer, photographed in the 1960s. *Flower Hill Foundation Collection.*

Opposite, bottom: The Flower Hill dining room was added in 1884. Jane Smoot updated her grandmother's wallpapers in 1959. This wallpaper pattern is titled the "Duke of Gloucester." *Flower Hill Foundation Collection.*

are drawn to the dining room with an oak dining table that extends to accommodate a dozen chairs. It is easy to envision Smoot family members, boarders, parishioners and friends seated here through the years, enjoying a simple meal and lively conversation.

"Mother always said that nobody would put his feet under her table who didn't work to earn it," Miss Jane Smoot shared in an oral history recording. "Each person at Flower Hill had specific responsibilities to help maintain the household. Another rule was that if anyone left food on a plate at the end of a meal, it would be covered and saved. That person would begin the next meal with that food before being allowed to partake in whatever else was served."

14

A family gathering on the original front porch, 1904. (*Left to right*) Lawrence Graham, Richmond Smoot, Asher Smoot, Sallie Smoot and Frances Sampson Smoot. *Flower Hill Foundation Collection.*

Jane Smoot welcomes guests to Flower Hill for a luncheon to celebrate the Texas Historic Medallion designation. *Flower Hill Foundation Collection.*

Miss Smoot, the last generation to live at Flower Hill, was dedicated to the task of collecting and preserving her family's history. We are the beneficiary of the rich story of three generations who influenced life in Austin—religion, education, law and journalism—beginning in 1877, when the city population was 11,013, and continuing until the death of Miss Smoot in 2013.

Regardless of the career pursuits of these erudite men and strong-willed, intelligent women, the Smoot family members shared respect for and an understanding of the importance of the written word. We are fortunate that this dynamic family of civil servants wrote and preserved many letters, essays and personal remembrances from which we can learn about their lives and be reminded of the transformation of Austin during the past century.

The narrative of this quietly influential Austin family is, to a great extent, told in their words, which easily relate the affection they shared, their work ethic and their steadfast commitment to public service.

Three Generations of the Smoot Family in Texas

Richmond Kelley Smoot
b. March 15, 1836
d. January 10, 1905
m. February 1, 1866
Sarah Jane "Sallie" Graham
b. April 21, 1837
d. December 22, 1916

Asher Graham Smoot
  b. August 28, 1869
  d. November 12, 1915
  m. February 18, 1903
Frances Sampson
  b. November 23, 1872
  d. September 29, 1934

Lawrence Kelley Smoot
  b. August 9, 1875
  d. June 29, 1968
  m. June 17, 1918
Julia Emma Williams
  b. September 19, 1883
  d. July 21, 1963

Jane Smoot
b. December 13, 1919
d. September 28, 2013

1
PREACHER, TEACHER AND PATRIARCH

DR. REVEREND RICHMOND SMOOT

*T*he Smoot family, whose roots were in Tennessee and Kentucky, came to Texas in 1876, a dozen years after the Civil War. Patriarch Richmond Kelley Smoot was born in 1836 in Huntingdon, Tennessee, and lived there until he attended Hanover College, a private liberal arts college in Indiana. After graduation in 1856, Richmond was licensed by the Presbytery of the Western District (Tennessee) in 1858 and ordained by the Presbytery of Muhlenberg, Kentucky, a year later. Following his graduation from the Danville Theological Seminary, Danville, Kentucky, in 1859, the Bowling Green, Kentucky Presbyterian Church installed Reverend Richmond Smoot as pastor.

Although the State of Kentucky tried to maintain neutrality during the Civil War, the Union army maintained a strong presence and the state eventually joined the Union. The Bowling Green Presbyterian Church Session Book recorded an example of Dr. Smoot's strong leadership during these devastating times. The entry is dated March 19, 1862.

Whereas since the middle of September last the town of Bowling Green has been occupied by a large army who invaded Kentucky from the South. During the whole time with a few rare exceptions, and amidst all the trials and difficulties which surrounded him, our minister, the Rev. R.K. Smoot, preached regularly every Sabbath and kept up the weekly prayer meeting. It is known that upon two occasions, at least, the medical department of the army had directed our church building to be occupied as a hospital, and

upon each occasion by a prompt and bold application in person to Gen.
Hardie, Rev. Smoot prevent[ed] said occupation and thus perhaps saved the
building from ruin. For these things, Rev. Smoot—and therefore, Resolved
that we, the members of his church hereby tender to him our thanks.

Sarah Jane Graham, known to friends and family as Sallie, regularly
attended the Presbyterian Church with her family, and during Richmond's
first years at the church, he began to court the spirited young woman.

On December 5, 1865, Reverend Smoot wrote a short letter to Sallie's
father asking for permission to marry his daughter:

Judge, Miss Sallie informs me that she has already communicated to you
the fact of an engagement and I write this note for the purpose of asking
your consent. It is our desire to consummate this engagement on the morning
of the first day of February, 1866, if your consent is given....I hope that
this announcement will meet your entire approbation. If so, please let me
hear from you by return mail if you can find time. Very truly, R.K. Smoot.

We do not have Mr. Graham's direct response to Richmond's appeal,
but this is a portion of a letter written on December 6, 1865, by Graham
to Sallie:

My dear daughter...I have received a note from Mr. Smoot. He seems to be
more timid than I had supposed him to be. I almost concluded to respond
to his inquiry by saying "my daughter is of full age, ask her," but upon
reflection, I suppose he has already asked you, and now I appoint you my
agent to say to him that I fully consent to the engagement, and shall not
interpose any objection. God help you, Arthur W. Graham

Richmond and Sallie were married on February 1, 1866. The groom
was thirty years old and the bride twenty-nine. Richmond had been paster
at Bowling Green Presbyterian Church for six years. During the next nine
years of their marriage, two sons were born: Asher Graham in 1869 and
Lawrence Kelley in 1875. The family lived in the small rectory adjoining
the church.

The Reverend Smoot received an honorary degree of Doctor of
Divinity from Southwestern University, Clarksville, Tennessee in 1875.
This honorary degree is traditionally granted to individuals who have
devoted their lives to theological pursuits or community betterment. In

Sallie Graham Smoot was born in 1837 in Bowling Green, Kentucky. *Flower Hill Foundation Collection.*

1889, he was elected to membership in the American Institute of Christian Philosophy with the degree of LLD.

Dr. Smoot first traveled to Austin, Texas, in July 1874, responding to a call to be pastor of the First Southern Presbyterian Church. However, upon his return to Bowling Green, a committee from that church met the train and announced that they would not release him to the Austin church. The minister also found that his wife was not agreeable to a move to Texas. She had lived in Kentucky her entire life and was strongly opposed to leaving her family.

At this time, the Austin church had just begun building a new structure, and only the foundation and walls were complete. According to a report from the First Southern Presbyterian Church elders, "Even though he was not yet free to accept the call, his visit to Austin did put new life into the congregation, and the church started a fund raising campaign to finish the structure."

In 1876, Dr. Smoot again petitioned the Bowling Green Presbyterian Church to dissolve his pastoral relation to the church, freeing him to accept the call to Austin. He wrote to the Kentucky congregation:

> *If I were to consult my own personal comforts, or if I were seeking merely a quiet pastorate among a devoted people, I would not go from this beautiful little city. But there are many reasons pressing upon me, like mighty convictions, which I cannot well throw into words, why I should not hesitate about accepting this call and entering at once upon this work... And I sincerely hope that you will not again put me to a severe test and a new trial by refusing to concur with me in seeking a dissolution of my pastoral relations when the path of duty appears so plain to me.... You must remember that this is the second time within the past two years that I have been constrained to bring this matter before you touching this same church* [Southern Presbyterian in Austin]. *Since the first day I visited that people I have had a strong desire to go and preach the Gospel to them.*

With a strong resolve and a wife who now supported the move, Dr. Smoot returned to Austin in 1876 and began a ministry that continued until his death in 1905. At the time of his arrival, the church was a small congregation with a sizeable debt. A notation in the January 18, 1882 church paper reported, "When Dr. Smoot came to this Church, five years ago, the number of members was 72. Since then, 75 have been dismissed or have died. And he has added 211 to the roll. When he took charge, the debt was $9,992.00. This is now being rapidly paid off by monthly subscriptions."

Left: Richmond Kelley Smoot, pictured here at age twenty-nine, was born in Huntingdon, Tennessee, in 1836. *Flower Hill Foundation Collection.*

Right: Sallie Graham Smoot is pictured here at the age of twenty-eight, the year before her marriage to Richmond Smoot. *Flower Hill Foundation Collection.*

Lawrence Smoot recalled family stories he was told about the move from Kentucky to Texas:

> *Of course, I remember nothing about that move, being just 14 months old. I later heard my parents tell about the trip which was a long, tedious one, consuming a week or more of time. The trains were slow and the connections—which usually resulted in a misconnection—were very bad, necessitating long waits at crossroad railroad stations. I heard them say that as we neared the Texas line, coming by way of New Orleans, which was the only railroad line running to Austin in those days, everybody began getting friendly as though they were all going to a common home. However, my mother in talking to one of the ladies on the train discovered that she [the other woman] was the wife of the new pastor of the Northern Presbyterian Church, in Austin, and the lady likewise discovered that my mother was the wife of the new pastor of Southern Presbyterian Church in Austin. As all of this was only a few years after the Civil*

War, which war split the Presbyterian Church so completely in two that the parts have not been welded together, it will be easy to understand why Dr. E.B. Wright and his family remained in their car and R.K. Smoot and his family remained in our car for the balance of the trip. We all detrained in Austin.

Upon their arrival in Austin, the Smoot family was met by a committee and escorted to the home of Mrs. C.R. Johns, where they lived in a small log house on the grounds of the main house, just east of the state capitol building, until their home on Pecan Street (now West Sixth Street) was complete.

Even with the promise of a new home, designed by her husband, the move from Kentucky to Texas must have been difficult for Sallie, who had deep roots in Bowling Green. Members of her family were leaders in that community. Arthur W. Graham, Sallie's father, was a circuit court judge, and he and his brother, John H. Graham, were clerks of session in the Presbyterian Church. In general, Sallie found that life in early Austin was often rough.

Years later, Lawrence wrote the following story as told to him by his mother:

A very notorious character who lived in Austin in those days was a man named Ben Thompson—good as gold at the heart, but quick as lightening [sic] at the trigger of his gun, and who would take no foolishness from any one. Most people liked him but it was too bad for the man that offered opposition to him. In those days the large majority of men carried six-shooters in their hip pockets and a dispute with a movement of the hand toward the hip pocket meant trouble in a hurry.

The night on which my father had his experience was Wednesday night immediately after prayer meeting. It was only a few days until Christmas and [eight-year-old] Asher had been begging for some firecrackers. After prayer meeting Papa had gone down on Congress Avenue to get these firecrackers for Asher. He got them and decided to walk up the Avenue and across the capitol yard to the cabin. He got the crackers and dropped them in the pocket of his sack coat. He always wore a sack coat and a little black string bow tie. Papa had only gone a short distance when a pistol cracked a block or so down the street. A second later the bullet whizzed through Papa's coat pocket, missing both his hand and his body, but setting off the package of firecrackers.

The next day it developed that someone had tried to get funny with Ben Thompson and the crack of the pistol was Thompson's answer. When Thompson heard about the firecrackers, he apologized to Papa and bought him a new coat; he also bought Asher some firecrackers.

First Southern Presbyterian Church located on the corner of Eighth and Brazos Streets, Austin, Texas. *Flower Hill Foundation Collection.*

Ben Thompson was elected Austin city marshal in 1881 and was killed by some "gangsters who had framed up against him" in San Antonio three years later. "Papa preached his funeral," Lawrence wrote.

During Richmond's ministry, the Southern Presbyterian Church was also called the Free Presbyterian Church. His granddaughter, Jane, explained in an oral history that "because of my grandfather's thinking and feelings, the church became unofficially known as the Free Church, or Free Presbyterian, since he would no longer accept the old colonial system of symbolically 'selling' pews to those members most financially able to pay large pledges."

Dr. Smoot provided leadership and a secure foundation for the Southern Presbyterian Church as a center of spirituality in the young city. The minister was said to have invaded every walk of life with his logic. A newspaper story stated, "There is no man in this state who has come into contact with his impressive personality who is not, and who has not been from that time, the better for it. Few men in Austin are better known and perhaps none enjoy a larger measure of public confidence."

Reverend Richmond Smoot, dedicated to his church and congregation, always kept the security and well-being of his beloved Sallie and his sons, Asher and Lawrence, a priority. He and Sallie set about to build a comfortable homeplace for their family that would also be an appropriate setting to meet the obligations of a minister and his wife.

Richmond recognized the promise of the fertile ground and a small lake with life-giving water on five acres on the far western edge of Austin. Sallie Smoot purchased the property in 1877 for $1,000 from Captain James H. Raymond, who originally bought the land from the Republic of Texas. Later that year, Sallie sold off a northern portion of the land to the Pillow family and used the proceeds to finance the construction of the Smoot home.

Set on a hill, the dignified four-room, two-story house, designed by Richmond and supervised by contractors R.J. Loving and W.M. Maxwell, cost $3,471.45. The Victorian Italianate style was popular at the time. A parlor, where the family also slept, and a dining room with a cross hall occupied the ground floor; a bedroom, reserved for guests, and Richmond's study were upstairs. A lattice breezeway led to a detached kitchen set just north from the main house. The original design of the house and later additions "cooperated" with nature, especially during the hot Texas summers. Cross halls and open windows allowed a breeze to cool the house naturally. The home did not have central air and heat until 2009.

Heirlooms and furniture from family homes in Tennessee and Kentucky, brought to Austin on the train, furnished the house. Many original chandeliers, eventually converted to electricity, are still in the home.

Carpenters working on the main house built a one-room, unpainted structure as a shelter and a place to store their tools. They intended to remove the small building when their work was finished. However, Dr. Smoot decided he could use it and paid them to leave it. This "lumber room" is still standing, which makes it the oldest structure on the property.

When construction began on the Smoot home, the western edge of Austin ran north and south along Shoal Creek to the river, and there were only four other residences in the rough scrub country west of Shoal Creek. In a 1940s essay, Lawrence Smoot described the area surrounding Flower Hill as an area where "the deer, the antelope, and the Indian had once had free range of the country." In a 1992 oral history interview, Richmond and Sallie's granddaughter, Jane Smoot, described the perimeter of the property: "It stretched from what is now West Sixth Street to West Ninth Street on the North; and it stretched from what is now Winflo Drive on the East to the midline of the property west of Pressler."

The east bedroom served as the childhood bedroom of Asher and Lawrence Smoot. Photograph by Robert Melton, 2019. *Flower Hill Foundation Collection.*

A July 27, 1877 newspaper article reported that "the water company finished laying pipes out Pecan street west as far as Pressler's brewery and James Johnson's, about one mile from the [Congress] Avenue." To induce the water company to extend pipes westward, property owners along the pipeline, including Richmond Smoot, each paid one hundred dollars. "Dr. Smoot and Marshal Purnell, we believe, contemplate building soon in the vicinity."

Robin Grace Soto, executive director of the Flower Hill Foundation, explained that once construction was underway, the "Butler Brick Company began using mule-drawn wagons to bring dusty rose-colored bricks, packed by hand from Colorado River mud, from Barton Springs and Zilker Park to the West Austin property. The bricks were made so quickly that the masons did not have time to form them smoothly in the brick molds before being sun-dried and fired in the kiln."

During an interview in October 1980, Jane Smoot explained that "in the late afternoon the way the sun slants, you can see hand prints and fingerprints all over those bricks." This witness to the handiwork accomplished over 140 years ago is still visible. Also visible are initials and signatures of family members and friends written on the exterior bricks through the years.

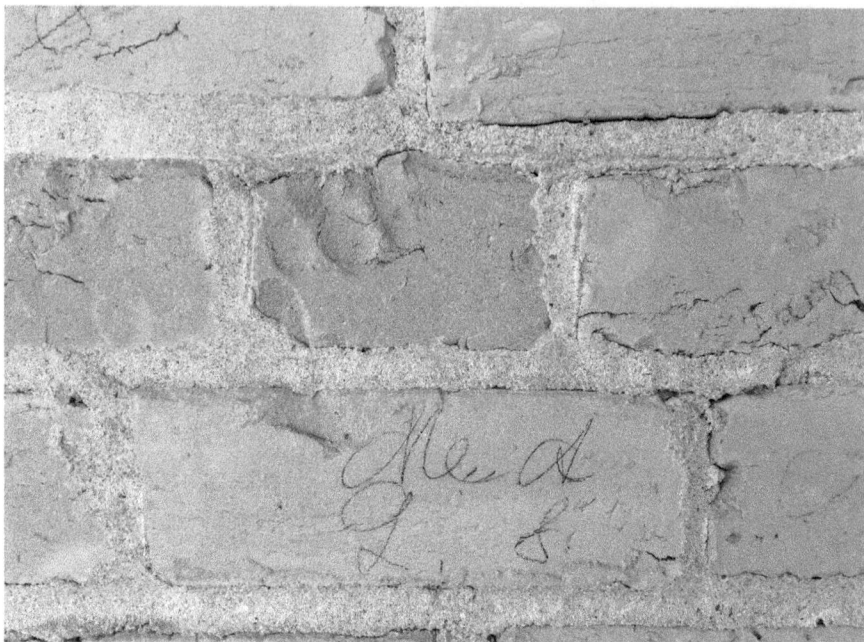

Handmade bricks from the Butler Brick Company of Austin were used to build Flower Hill. Family members and guests signed the bricks during visits. *Flower Hill Foundation Collection.*

A letter dated October 30, 1877, from Richmond in Austin to Sallie, who was visiting a cousin in San Antonio, gave this update on the construction of their home:

> *This afternoon Asher and I drove out to the house together, and the men are tinning it, but they are not getting on very fast. The stairsteps are all done and ready to put up. Mr. Loving* [the contractor] *is doing a great deal of the work in the shop and so the house is getting on faster than it appears to be....We miss you and Lawrence very much. God bless you. Our love to all. Your own R.K.S.*

Sallie wrote to "Dear Chick" (her pet name for Richmond) the next day describing her trip with Lawrence in the stagecoach on its regular run from Austin to San Antonio:

> *I wrote you a postal yesterday, which announced our safe arrival. The roads were very rough and we were in suspense all the way as to whether we*

would make the connections, which as I wrote you, we only made by a few minutes. I fear you will have a hard time to get over for it has been raining most of the time since I have been here. I expect the roads will be fearful. If it continues to rain, you will have to go around by Houston I expect.

The baby [Lawrence] is well and misses Papa and Ash. Tell Asher I think of him often, and miss my dear boy, and hope he will be a good boy and keep well. Look on the mantel, behind the brass lamp, and you will find that box of ointment, bring it with you, as I want it for Lawrence's ears. Kiss Ash for Lawrence and Mama, and imagine one for yourself, from Lawrence and Sallie.

A response dated November 1, 1877, from Richmond related that the contractor had told him that the house would be done and ready for him to "receive" on the tenth day of November:

He says we can move in, if we are ready, next Monday week. He has made out a complete diagram of the rooms above and below and brought it to me so that I may mail it to you to have the carpets cut. [Sallie's San Antonio relative was in the carpet business.] *I will bring it over with me. You can select them [carpets] before I come and have them cut as soon as I do come and then we can send them on ahead of us by Express so that they may be here when we get home. I am as anxious to get in as he is to get his money. He says he needs the money and so he is going to put all his hands on my house. He told me to tell you to get ready to move in....Affectionately yours, R.K. Smoot*

From 1882 through 1884, additions were made to the house at Flower Hill, including a library/study, a small latticed porch on the north side of the library and a bedroom upstairs. During this time, the Smoots joined the kitchen to the house and added a bathroom and pantry between the kitchen and the dining room. Lawrence Smoot explained in his remembrances that this room arrangement was Sallie Smoot's idea so there would be a buffer between the kitchen and the family dining room to "prevent the servants in the kitchen from hearing the conversation during meals."

A porch to the north and east of the kitchen was installed. At some point, a large cellar, hewn out of bedrock, was excavated under the house. Telephone lines were installed in the early 1880s.

A curving carriage drive of gravel and small rocks, designed to prevent erosion, was added to the property in the early 1900s. Later a concrete surface was installed to the drive, and curbing was added. This narrow drive served a practical purpose but also added visual interest to the property.

"After Grandfather bought the place and they began to develop and tame it into a civilized form from the original roughness, Grandmother seems to have had considerable skill in growing plants. So much so that she is the one responsible for naming the place Flower Hill," Miss Smoot explained.

This story is a family joke. Grandfather had not known pecans in Kentucky, and oh, he did like those pecans when he came to Texas. He was so enamored of pecans that he was intent on naming the homeplace Pecan Place. Oddly enough, none grew here in the native original on the place, so Grandfather began trying to make pecans grow here. I'm guessing he planted other people's pecans, or he may have dug up young trees and brought them here. He had a dreadful time, and the trees weren't surviving.

In those days houses were named, there were no numbers, there was not even a street [in front of the property], *it was just a road. Grandfather could not make the pecans grow, and Grandmother was doing remarkably well with flowers of all sorts. She, in a teasing way, suggested that he give up on the pecans and call the place Flower Hill because her flowers were blooming all over the hill. Of course, now we have pecan trees, but those were put out by my father.*

Some of the original fruit trees, planted in the early days, still thrive. "They didn't plant the fruit trees in strict orchard rows, but instead spotted them here, there, and yonder, to look pretty as well as produce fruit," Jane said. "Some of the fig trees are still here and the wild plums."

Unfortunately, the idyllic lake setting at Flower Hill was short-lived. Richmond had to eliminate the lake to appease a troublesome, demanding neighbor. "A family moved in up on the hill, and when they moved in the woman of the family was sickly," Miss Smoot related. "She had one thing after another plus some more, but she took it into her head that Dr. Smoot's lake was causing all of her trouble. She began complaining about the lake. Grandfather is said to have told her that none of us is sick and no one else around here is sick; and 'pardon me, but you were sick when you came here.' It was a clean body of water with fish in it. However, the neighbor kept on and finally I guess Grandfather got tired of her nagging and had the hill cut out, eliminating the lake. The natural spring then formed a creek where there is now a street. It was a pretty little creek and I remember playing along it." The "little creek" was directed into a six-foot sewer down the middle of Pressler, across West Sixth Street, through low-level lots and on into Lady Bird Lake.

The Smoot's younger son, Lawrence, wrote in later years about his early memories of the Flower Hill neighborhood:

> *Being of tender years (2 years) when we moved to our new home, I do not recall the many things that no doubt happened in those early days. As years went by I do recall the Old Pressler Garden which was across the road and about a city block further to the West. It was a beer garden with a saloon facing the road and some three acres of land to the south extending to the railroad tracks. A portion of this was a large grove of elm threes which furnished a fine picnic and resting place, while further south was an open field devoted to games and baseball.*
>
> *On Sunday afternoons this was the gathering place and the mode of entertainment was a brass band which furnished music from about 2 o'clock in the afternoon until near sunset. After dark the string band would take over and play as long as there were any dancers. We enjoyed this very much. In fact, we looked forward to it. It made Asher mad as thunder for anything to happen on Sunday afternoon that would necessitate his having to leave home, so he could not listen to the band.*

During the years that her husband served as minister of a growing church congregation, Sallie kept the household operating smoothly and fulfilled the responsibilities expected of a minister's wife. She helped organize the Women's Home and Foreign Missionary Society in 1896. The group met monthly to study foreign and home missions of the church.

The sweeping landscape of Flower Hill was often the setting of social gatherings. The July 3, 1904 edition of the Austin paper described such an event:

> *The lawn party given by the ladies of the Free Presbyterian Church Tuesday evening at the home of their pastor, Dr. Smoot, was a very pleasant affair in every particular. The lawn was invitingly arranged with rugs, garden seats, and cushions, lighted brightly with colored lanterns. Delicious cake and cream were dispensed by the affable hostesses, who were untiring in their efforts to afford all the guests a delightful time.*

For many years, Sallie Smoot was also well regarded in Austin for her willingness to share the bounty of the beautiful flower gardens that surrounded the family home. At the time, there was only one florist in

In 1907, Sallie Graham Smoot sat for this portrait in her bedroom at Flower Hill. The photograph was taken by her son Lawrence. *Flower Hill Foundation Collection.*

Austin, owned by the Hillyers family. Occasionally, the demand for flowers at one time—for funerals, weddings and other special events—was more than the florist could handle. Mr. Hillyers would come to Flower Hill, and Sallie would share whatever was blooming at the time. The minister's wife also regularly furnished flowers for the church.

As minister of the Southern Presbyterian Church, Dr. Smoot was often intimately involved in the lives of his congregation and, at times, called on to help members of the Austin community who were not members of his church.

An essay written by Lawrence Smoot in the 1940s gives us his observations of his father's life in the spiritual service of others. Given Dr. Smoot's devotion to his congregation and considering their expressions of loyalty and affection for their minister through the years, Dr. Smoot's view of his service during this time would most likely be very different from his son's.

> *While Papa was a preacher and gave his full time to it, that profession, in his day, was not at all remunerative. It seemed that the members of his church thought he could live on air, love, hope, and faith. Or, possibly they*

could have that, being a preacher, God would sustain him and his family without their eating or having clothes to wear. Although they promised him a regular salary, it was seldom paid. Yet, there was no hesitation on their part in calling upon him in cases of sickness or death among the members of his congregation. Or to preach a funeral or perform a marriage ceremony at any time regardless of time whether it be day or night, but few concerned themselves in any attempt to see that his salary was paid.

Well do I remember that one cold winter morning along about three o'clock, with the thermometer somewhere near the freezing point, that I jumped out of bed and threw a bath robe around me to answer the front door bell. When I opened the door, a man, so wrapped up in his overcoat that only his nose and eyes were visible, announced that his sister's baby was dying and they wanted Papa to come and baptize it immediately—and Papa went. Two days later he went again to preach the baby's funeral.

Another time, when we were out in the chicken yard, building a coop for a new brood of baby chicks, a city carriage drove up, and the driver announced that he had been sent to drive Dr. Smoot to a funeral of a young child, the father and mother of which were members of the church. Papa did not even know the child had been sick—but Papa went.

On another occasion—a bleak November day—Papa had a bad cold and had just made himself comfortable in his study, before a warm fire, with a favorite book in his hand and the medicine bottle on a table by his side, hoping to eliminate the cold. The telephone rang and the party at the other end of the wire told him that a young man—a University student and an attendant upon our church—was quite sick at his rooming house and needed some spiritual uplifting. Notwithstanding Papa's physical feelings, he dressed and went as far as the street car would take him and then walked four blocks, through a drizzling rain, to the young man's boarding house only to find that the young man in question had gone to a football game.

These incidents were only a few that helped describe the life of a preacher of that day.

Dr. Reverend Smoot was well known, well liked and perhaps a bit of a romantic, making him a favorite to perform wedding ceremonies. Lawrence was a firsthand witness to many of these events:

As for weddings, Papa's only mission was to perform the ceremony. That did not take but a few minutes of his time, so the people said. Whether or not it was convenient for the preacher was a small matter, he had nothing else to do when Cupid shot his arrow, but to tie the knot. The time of day and place or circumstance made no difference. Church weddings, as a rule, were for the members and were arranged for some days in advance, so the church could be decorated. Others were not so exacting, but when the lady said, "Yes," the groom, or one of his friends, would rush off to the county clerk's office, or, if it should be at night, to the home of the county clerk, to get the marriage license, and then rush out to the preacher's home, not knowing whether he was there or not, or having dinner with his family, to have the knot tied, muy pronto.

On many occasions the door bell would clang out on a still night—around midnight or even later—for some young couple to get married. Papa would throw on his dressing gown, go to the door, invite the young people into the parlor, perform the ceremony, receive his fee—which was usually more liberal than church contributions—close the door, and return to his bed, without even knowing who the parties were, except for the names they gave in introducing themselves and written on the marriage license. There was no law that fixed the fee for a marriage ceremony. It was just what the groom was able to put up at the time, ranging from two or three dollars to one hundred.

Romance, as generally understood, applies to lovers and young married people, but sometimes its effect rebounds upon the preacher and his family. At least they get a good deal of "kick" out of it. Sometimes family members were the witnesses for the wedding. A number of times I was the goat on a cold night to answer the doorbell, or I went out to unhitch the horse, so Papa could get into the house to the fire after a long drive home from a wedding.

On one occasion Papa was asked to go to the country to marry a young couple, the bride being the daughter of a wealthy cattleman. The night was cold with a strong north wind blowing. Papa took a heavy blanket for his buggy robe, but the cold wind was very cutting on his face. I went out and helped him unharness the horse and feed her, but it was too cold for conversation so little was said until we reached the house. Then he shared his experience. After the wedding was over and Papa was ready to start home, the young groom went with him to his buggy, helped him get up into it, and with the remark "these might help you in driving," handed Papa a pair of fur-lined gloves, which Papa threw into the bottom of the buggy because he had his regular driving gloves on his hands. Papa said that he would much rather have the price of those gloves in cash than to *have the gloves. As he walked into the warmth of home, he handed the gloves to Mama and said, "Here's your fee." It was the custom in those days for a preacher to give his wife all of the wedding fees. Mama, with a disappointed look on her face, looked at the gloves, turned them over a time or two, then tried one of them on. As her fingers ran into the glove, she jerked it off and said, "What is this?" An investigation revealed a five dollar gold piece in each finger of each glove.*

Following one late night spontaneous wedding ceremony in the parlor, as the couple was leaving the groom pressed something hard against the palm of Papa's hand. Papa did not look at it, but closed the door and went upstairs. Mama was in bed asleep so, without disturbing her, he slipped the coin into her dresser drawer, assuming that it was a twenty dollar gold coin. Upon arising the next morning, Mama picked up her wedding fee only to find that it was a 'drink check' on the Iron Front Saloon—one of the most popular saloons and gambling houses in Austin at the time. Papa offered to take the check to the saloon and cash it.

John Neff, the owner of the saloon, was a good friend of Papa's and happened to be standing in front of his place of business the morning Papa walked up the street. As usual in passing, Papa stopped and spoke to Mr. Neff, and added, "John, I have a check on your bank that I would like for you to cash." Mr. Neff, without any sign of surprise said, "Alright doctor, this is a good check, but it will have to be cashed over the bar." "Lead the way," Papa replied. Mr. Neff made good on the check, handing Papa twenty-five dollars in cash.

The nocturnal and unexpected weddings were often for honest, hard working boys and girls. Some of them, after a hard days' work would decide that they could make a better living going in double harness than they could as it was. They would decide to get married that night and both go back to work the next morning, as though nothing had happened. Many a time as Papa started out the front door to go to prayer meeting, a couple would be at the door asking to get married. He would marry them and they would all go to prayer meeting together.

Characterizations of Dr. Smoot as a persuasive, powerful orator combined with vintage, somber photographs give the false impression that this minister was a conventional "fire and brimstone" preacher. However, along with a commanding presence, Reverent Smoot possessed the sincere ability to communicate with, and empathize with, all ages and all types of individuals. This passage from an 1891 baccalaureate address delivered at

Dr. Reverend Richmond Kelley Smoot, pastor of the First Southern Presbyterian Church, also known as Free Presbyterian Church, Austin, Texas. *Flower Hill Foundation Collection.*

Poltier College, Bowling Green, Kentucky, illustrates his ability to appreciate the experiences of youth:

> *The young look forward—there is no past to them. In the morning of life the sun rises clear and bright. The landscape is bathed in the freshness of youth and beauty. The brain and the heart both, busy as the bee, are gathering sweetness from everything around. It is grand to live. Life has rolled no heavy burden on the soul. Every prospect charms the eye, and the future is as full of hopes as the firmament is of stars when the night is clear. In life's early morning the imagination spreads her broad canvas.*

Dr. Smoot's service and recognition were not confined to the purview of First Southern Presbyterian Church. He was a noted presence in the Central Texas Presbytery and, with Reverend W.F. Gillespie, was present in 1877 when eight members organized a church in Round Rock, Texas. He served as chaplain for the Texas Senate from 1882 to 1891, "invoking the blessings of the Divine Being upon the deliberations of the body." He was moderator of the Presbyterian General Assembly meeting in Atlanta, Georgia, in 1882, the first Texas Presbyterian so honored. In 1889, he was appointed to the Board of Prison Appraisers by Texas governor Joseph Sayers. He also offered dedicatory prayers for laying the cornerstone of Old Main at The University of Texas and the dedication of the state capitol building.

Perhaps most demanding on Dr. Smoot's intellect and time outside of his ministerial responsibilities was his creation and administration of the

Austin School of Theology to train young men to become ministers. Local church history asserted that "Dr. Rev. Smoot's greatest accomplishment was his leadership in theological education in Austin."

In 1882, at the request of his associates in Texas, Dr. Smoot began training aspiring students who wished to study personally under the coaching of an established minister. The first student to apprise himself of this highly specialized education rendered in the Smoot home library was William Stuart Red. After completing his studies at the Austin School of Theology, he taught Hebrew there until 1888. During the following years, Reverend Red served several Presbyterian churches in Texas, including the Bee Cave Presbyterian Church near Austin (1920–23).

As interest in Dr. Smoot's efforts increased, Dr. Robert L. Dabney, a longtime faculty member of the Union Theological Seminary in Virginia, joined the Austin seminary faculty. Both men taught classes but received no compensation. Enrollment increased, and classes were moved to the basement of the First Southern Presbyterian Church. The rapid growth of the Presbyterian Church in the Southwest fostered the need for ministers. For eleven years, the Austin School of Theology helped meet that need; however, Dr. Smoot was unable to sustain the seminary due to a period of economic uncertainty. When the school closed in 1895, it had trained forty-four ministers.

In the book *Story of the First Southern Presbyterian Church Austin, Texas*, commemorating the first one hundred years of the church, William A. McLeod, DD, explained how the assets of two Austin educational establishments, Stuart Seminary and Austin School of Theology, contributed to the founding of Austin Presbyterian Theological Seminary. When the Stuart Seminary for Girls, founded by Rebecca Red, closed in 1899, the Red family heirs, "assisted by certain funds salvaged by Dr. R.K. Smoot from the assets of the old Austin School of Theology, were able to present to the Synod of Texas for a Theological Seminary, the fine school property. Here the new Austin Presbyterian Theological Seminary began its work on October 1, 1902, this writer being one of the six students there." In 1907, the property was sold. After several transfers, in 1926, it was acquired by the Catholic Diocese of Galveston.

Austin Presbyterian Theological Seminary is now located at 100 East Twenty-Seventh Street. Dr. Smoot served on the Board of Trustees of the seminary from its organization until his election as professor of church history and government. He served in that capacity from October 1903 until his death. First Southern Presbyterian Church history relates that when Dr.

Smoot was elected to this chair, "the position was without endowment, and so, lacking in funds to pay the salary. It was, therefore, provided that he should still retain, for the time, his pastorate."

As a balance to his pastoral and teaching responsibilities, Dr. Smoot enjoyed the rural quality of life at Flower Hill on the western edge of Austin. From the beginning, the Smoots kept horses to use with the carriages and buggies. "Grandfather used a rather small buggy. It was easy to handle and quick to get going. There was also a carriage for the family use and a sulky which was not much more than a seat balanced between two wheels, for racing purposes," Jane Smoot explained. "As Daddy grew older he raised some fine horses. My Grandmother was from Kentucky and devoted to horses and I believe Daddy got his appreciation from her."

In addition to the horses, there were, at various times, cows, pigs, ducks, chickens and guineas. "There were some deer, too," Jane said. "Daddy remembered that when Grandfather would go hunting, sometimes he would come across a motherless fawn, and he would bring it home and hand-feed it."

To supplement his salary as a minister, Richmond often employed a practice that his son Lawrence called "In and Out Calves." Dr. Smoot's granddaughter, Jane, described the process:

> *Most people in town had a milk cow and when the cows would come in fresh with new calves, they didn't want to keep the calves. Once the calves were weaned, the owner was keen to get rid of them. Of course, everyone knew everyone else, and when Grandfather knew someone had a fresh cow and the calf was about weaning stage, he'd drive by in his buggy and offer to buy the calf for a couple of dollars. Grandpa had bought a stretch of land in Hayes County at a very good price because most didn't see any worth in the cedar breaks and rocky land of the countryside. He fenced the area and put in a windmill. Then [he] would buy all the calves he could. He would keep them on that land until he was sure they were self-sufficient, on a grazing land. In due time my Grandfather would have a ranch stocked with cattle that he could sell at considerable profit. In those days, ministers were expected to do something on the side, not just sit up in a beautiful office and get a big check. They had to make a living some other way.*

Lawrence explained that the ranch was a perfect way for his father to enjoy the outdoors and spend time away from Flower Hill, where he was often interrupted by someone seeking spiritual counsel or some other service of a minister.

We had a large back lot in which the calves could run, but that brought up the feed question for us. The ranch was the answer. I'm not sure how profitable Papa's ranching endeavors were. I think that at the bottom of the whole thing Papa was about as interested in the fishing that Onion Creek, near the ranch, if not more so, than he was in the cattle business. Sometimes he would stay two or three days. Mama did not like it because she thought the area of the ranch was a hideout for robbers and cut-throats. She was in constant fear that someone would hurt him. Eventually he sold out the ranch business.

Dr. Smoot didn't procure all of his calves from neighbors. The *Austin Weekly Statesman* reported on September 2, 1880, that "Rev. Dr. Smoot of this city received a few mornings ago, by the International Express, one of the prettiest short horn heifer calves ever imported into this state. It was a present from Mr. Alfred Simmons, one of the well known breeders of Kentucky thoroughbred short horn cattle. The calf is three months old, a dark mahogany red and a model of beauty."

Dr. Smoot loved hunting, fishing and outdoor life in general. Lawrence believed that his father received inspiration from the open field that helped him develop Bible lessons and illustrations to use in his sermons. "His experiences in the outdoors provided a common subject for conversation and no doubt was one of the reasons for his popularity among different classes of people." The following description written in an essay by Lawrence highlights the popularity of his father:

On summer nights when all the church windows were open during services, passersby would notice large numbers of people—mostly men—quietly seated on the grass in the shadows, listening to Papa's sermons. These people frequently out numbered those on the inside. By the time the service was over and those on the inside came out all of these lawn sitters would be gone. They were a group of people that lived the night life and not in accordance with the strict ideas of the usual church goer.

Another habit that perhaps added to Papa's popularity was that when he finished a conversation and was about to leave, regardless of who he was talking with, his parting sentence was, "Come hear me preach."

Among the countless weddings conducted in the parlor of Flower Hill by Reverend Smoot, one, in particular, was well-remembered by fourteen-year-old Lawrence. He and his mother were sitting on the porch one night waiting for Dr. Smoot to return from a church meeting. "It was very hot and we had lit no lamps in the house because the burning kerosene only added to the oppressive heat." After his father arrived at home, the family continued to sit on the porch, delaying going indoors. Lawrence remembered that it was approximately 10:30 p.m. when they heard a team of horses crossing the wooden bridge that spanned Shoal Creek. "I remember Mama saying that this must be a wedding and that Papa had come home just in time."

One of the Smoot's Pecan Street neighbors parked the carriage at the gate and walked toward the house. He explained that he had a couple in the carriage who wished to get married.

> *Papa asked the names of the couple, and Mr. Anderson answered, "Will Porter and Athol Estes."*
>
> *Papa told him to bring them in. He recognized the names of members of the church. Both sang in the choir, and they had visited our home. Everybody knew Will Porter and Athol Estes were in love, but they were both in such poor health we didn't think anything would come of it. Mr. Porter had tuberculosis and had come to Austin for his health. I remember that Miss Estes was a pretty girl, not strikingly beautiful, but pretty.*

The elopement of Will Porter and Athol Estes on June 1, 1887, caused quite a stir, as the bride's mother had chosen another, wealthy, man for her daughter. She very much opposed the marriage to Porter, who at the time was employed at the Harrell Cigar Store located in the Driskill Hotel.

Porter eventually became a well-known writer whose pen name was O. Henry. He is best known for his short story "The Gift of the Magi."

Although Sallie Smoot had moved far away from her family, she remained loyal and communicated regularly with them. According to young Lawrence, Sallie's brother, Lawrence's mercantile business in Bowling Green had "gone broke, and Mama felt sorry for him. And Papa felt sorry for Mama, with the result that Papa offered Uncle Lawrence a proposition to come to Austin. That was when our hard luck began, and our home became crowded."

Sallie's brother, Lawrence Graham, moved to Austin in 1889 with his daughter, Lena, and two sons. His sons soon moved to San Antonio, but except for a short time, Lena lived with her father at Flower Hill until he died in 1917.

When these relatives moved into Flower Hill, the two Lawrences became roommates—sharing a bed in the upstairs bedroom. "That went on for a year or more when my health began to break down and we did not know why," Lawrence explained. "When our family physician came out to the house one day to see me, he discovered that Uncle Lawrence was my roommate. He told Papa that that was the cause of my trouble. The doctor believed that because Uncle Lawrence was so much older than I, that he was sapping all of my strength. He advised that we have separate beds if not separate rooms."

Richmond and Sallie's solution reveals their respectful attitude toward family members, even at their own expense and convenience. Rather than present the problem to the elder Lawrence and risk causing hard feelings, they decided to add a room to the second floor and make him think that he should no longer live in crowded conditions with his nephew but should have a room to himself. "The only place availing was the top of the dining room, so off came the roof and up went Uncle Lawrence's new bedroom."

"Papa had done fairly well with his trades in lands and cattle, but now he planted it all in the mercantile business. Uncle Lawrence and his children were to furnish the experience and do the work." Graham & Co. opened on Congress Avenue, but with his experience limited to a similar business in Kentucky, Uncle Lawrence had difficulty offering an inventory that appealed to his Austin customers. The business was not successful.

Dr. Reverend Richmond Smoot died suddenly of heart failure at home on January 10, 1905. He was sixty-eight years old. The newspaper obituary stated: "He had been at his place in the Theological Seminary on Saturday, and on Sabbath morning and night had filled his pulpit and preached with accustomed power and impressiveness. During the previous week of prayer he had been present at every service, and on Friday night had closed the series of meetings with a very tender and helpful and impressive address."

One of the four ministers who conducted Dr. Smoot's memorial service described him as "one of the greatest of Southern ministers. He always examined the new but always held totally devoted to the entire faith in Almighty God." Another remembered him as "a forceful preacher that crowds came to hear. All pews full, and chairs in the aisles, when he preached." Others described Dr. Smoot in condolence letters as a "sympathetic pastor, an eloquent preacher, a profound thinker, and, above all, he was truly a great man. No man can be truly great who isn't truly good."

Sallie Smoot lived at Flower Hill with her son Lawrence until her death on December 22, 1916. Called "a lovely Christian character" by a former minister, she was honored in the First Southern Presbyterian Church bulletin at the time of her death: "For 28 years in this city, she was a silent partner

Richmond and Sallie Smoot on their thirty-seventh wedding anniversary, February 1, 1903. Photograph taken by their son, Lawrence. *Flower Hill Foundation Collection.*

and a true helpmate to her husband, the beloved pastor of this Church for these years. Since his death in 1905, she has been a faithful member and worker in this organization, so doubly dear to her. Till failing health came, then final release from earthly labor."

A common trait that ran true through all three generations of the Smoot family was the precise handling of their personal affairs. A clear example of this is a letter written by Sallie to her son Lawrence a few weeks before she died. She requested a plain, simple service at Flower Hill and detailed the clothes in which to bury her. "The present church membership are mostly strangers to me, so take me from the home I love so well, and lay me beside your Papa. You will find sufficient funds to meet all expenses in the trunk in my room upstairs." Sallie instructed Frankie (her daughter-in-law) and Lena Graham (her niece) to look at her clothes and take anything they could use. "Put what they don't want in the cedar chest with your Papa's clothes."

She also wrote that she wanted Lawrence "to marry as soon as you can arrange to do so. I had always hoped to be here to make the house attractive and give your wife a mother's greeting, but that is not to be, for I find I am losing strength day by day. You have been a comfort from the time of your Papa's death and since Asher was taken from us, you have been all to me. I trust the Lord has many rich blessings in store for you, and that your future life may be full of good things."

2

LONG-HAIRED POET OF THE *AMERICAN-STATESMAN*

ASHER GRAHAM SMOOT

orn in Bowling Green, Kentucky, in 1869, Asher was eight years old when the Richmond Smoot family moved to Austin. The boy's early education was at the Texas German-English Academy, taught by Jacob Bickler, in the structure historically known as the Wahrenberger House near the state capitol. Later he attended The University of Texas and began to make his mark as a journalist for the *Democratic Statesman* when he was seventeen years old.

Lawrence Smoot, six years younger than his brother, shared a childhood memory in a personal essay written in 1947:

> *Most of the country* [surrounding Flower Hill] *was at our disposal and as soon as we were old enough, Papa taught us both how to shoot. Asher had a small shotgun. I used a cap pistol for a long time, then a small rifle.*
>
> *Our school was some two miles from home. Asher rode a little black Spanish pony named Diamond—a regular little devil—but he and Asher got along fine. In fact, Asher seemed to be a part of the pony when on his back. I sat behind Asher going to and from school, except when Diamond decided that two was one too many, and while poking along, apparently half asleep, would suddenly start into action, leaving me suspended in midair until gravity rapidly pulled me to the ground. By the time Asher could get the pony under control and come back to where I was, I had usually recovered myself sufficiently to arise to my feet rubbing a rather*

Asher Graham Smoot photographed on the original front porch of Flower Hill by his brother, Lawrence. *Flower Hill Foundation Collection.*

painful posterior. Asher, knowing I was not seriously injured, would laugh, and Diamond would have the most pathetic look, as if to say "did it hurt you?" I would manage to get back up on his back and we would continue our ride. I often wonder if that is why my hips hurt so often now!

Asher lived with his family at Flower Hill until he married Frances Sampson, daughter of a prominent Austin family, on February 18, 1903.

The community-minded young man, who became known by his initials "A.G.," was a member of the Austin Lodge of Elks and the Austin Chamber of Commerce, and he served as president of the Austin Business League. Asher was chairman of the reception committee and a prominent participant in a carriage procession when President Teddy Roosevelt visited Austin in 1905. He was also a charter member and director of the Rotary Club of Austin. That organization published a moving resolution honoring Asher after his death, describing him as "one of our most active and useful members who became favorably known throughout the state through his public service." The resolution continues to note Asher's service to the organization and community, closing with: "He was ever interested in the welfare of this city and society mourns for one who, by his gracious, kindly bearing, brought pleasure wherever he appeared."

Judging from the many mentions of Richmond and Sallie's older son on the society pages of the Austin, San Antonio, and Houston newspapers, Asher was a popular guest at many soirees. Both as a single young man and after his marriage to Frances, Asher was often in the center of the social circle of Austin. Many midnight picnics, early suppers followed by dancing and galas regularly included the name "A.G. Smoot" among the attendees. Two card games, whist and euchre, were trendy, and the Young Ladies Afternoon Whist Club No. 1 elevated the games to a more sophisticated level with elegant suppers. The older Smoot son was a coveted guest at these gatherings. A few times, it was noted that "regretfully A.G. Smoot was not in attendance."

A.G. Smoot and his wife, Frances Sampson Smoot, were often guests at the governor's mansion. These events were usually social with an underlying political purpose; however, a New Year's Eve gala hosted by Governor and Mrs. Thomas Campbell must have been especially grand. Frances's gown made the news alongside the description of the governor's wife's "lavender czarina satin gown, embroidered in gold and trimmed in rose point. Mrs. A.G. Smoot wore a blue satin evening gown, trimmed with silver applique and spangles."

Lawrence Smoot respected the many differences between him and his brother and wrote admiringly:

> *He was born at night, I in the day time, and that was about the way it stayed all along the line. In my brother's early days at school he developed a talent for writing compositions, he wrote a good hand while mine looked like turkey tracks made in a hurry. My compositions were very uninteresting. I could not get the hang of swinging words into line so that they would sound sensible, while all he had to do was pick up a pen and words flowed onto the page.*

Richmond and Sallie's older son became well known and respected as a journalist with a reputation for cheerful optimism, an uncommon attitude for a newspaperman of the time. He often used popular political cartoon characters to express clever observations on political matters and politicians. A colleague with the *Houston Post* once described Asher as "the long-haired poet of the *Statesman*."

Asher left the *Democratic Statesman* in 1911, when the paper changed owners, to work as a correspondent and freelance writer. Three years later, he cofounded the *Austin American* newspaper in partnership with Henry

Asher Smoot (*standing*) and (*left to right*) Mrs. M.G. Sanderson, George Nalle and Frances Sampson Smoot. *Flower Hill Foundation Collection.*

H. Sevier, another seasoned newspaper professional. Sevier's wife, the former Miss Clara Driscoll, helped provide financial backing for the new enterprise. The *Austin American* published daily, including Sunday, and the first edition printed on May 31, 1914. Introduced as "the capital city's new daily," the newspaper was considered a credit to Texas journalism due to the reputation of Sevier and Smoot. "The *American* dedicates its best efforts to the upbuilding, progress, and prosperity of Austin." By April 1915, the average daily distribution was 11,239. Austin population was 32,200.

Letters to his seventy-eight-year-old mother, written in large, sprawling handwriting, reveal a close, affectionate relationship between the two. On the envelope holding this December 7, 1913 letter, from the Hotel Knickerbocker in New York, Sallie noted "a precious letter from my boy":

Dearest Mama, I kept my promise today and went to church this morning though to do it I had to go five blocks through a heavy rain and I don't know whether I got into the right kind of Presbyterian church or whether I fell into the hands of the Yankees. At any rate the preacher put up a strong talk for money for foreign missionary work and that made me feel at home especially when ten elderly men began passing the plates to get this missionary money.

He got a good deal too. There were lots of one dollar bills and some five dollar bills dropped in, in my neighborhood, but I couldn't go any stronger than 25 cents. The old gentlemen passing the plates kept covering all the small change with the bills. I presume for the effect it might have in making others dig but there wasn't anything in my pocket to dig so it was love's labor lost on me. I didn't like the fellow's sermon much. He must be one of the revised Bible advocates. At least to my idea he was weak on his orthodox. His intentions were evidently good but his information is bad. Even I know that.

I am enclosing you a program. It has been raining hard ever since daylight and it is a dark, gloomy day. I came from church, got my dinner and I am going to stay in my room this afternoon with nothing but my thoughts for company and they are not of the best I can assure you.

That church this morning opened afresh the book for me at pages that have been closed save in memory and while you and Lawrence seem able to do your duty by the present I must admit that I cannot as the attempt opens afresh wounds that are always bleeding but which I can control somewhat if I do not let myself think, but today as upon other days when I have tried to do my duty, I find the flesh willing but the spirit far too weak.

The only way I can control myself is to get away from myself and force myself to think of other things. Naturally you can appreciate my feelings of today but I had no business telling them to you save that a boy of 44 years must go to somebody sometime and in my case I turn to my mother, knowing that she won't judge me harshly when others do. With much love I am Lovingly Asher.

The following, written on Vanderbilt Hotel, New York City letterhead, is dated June 1915:

Dear Mama: We arrived here early this afternoon after a rather tiresome hot trip, barring the nights, all the way up. On the level now, I kept well and in good shape all the way—in fact I am in better shape than any of the rest....George [a young nephew] *is complaining slightly of a stomachache and Frankie* [pet name for his wife, Frances] *has her troubles about everybody being dirty.*

I had one depressing day up, when I didn't feel so good on account of the heat, but I am ok today with a great big OK for sure, but I am not bragging. If I get to feeling bad, I will let you know (honest) so if you do not hear from me to the effect that I am, you may know that I feel fine and am rushing Broadway good and plenty.

Love to all. Tell the kid [Lawrence] *the next trip here is to be with you, the kid, and myself. If we can't get you here any other way we will bring you here for a medical examination and the prescription will be that you will have to spend two weeks sightseeing...spend a week in the botanical gardens at the zoo. Do Broadway at night, shoot the shoots at Coney Island, eat a $10.00 dinner in a big hotel where there isn't much to eat but plenty pay. Ride taxi cabs, go to the theatres and moving pictures shows, ocean trips to points around New York and etc...all with the personal supervision and control of your oldest son and you to make no attempt at managing anything! Lovingly, Ash*

Asher and Frances had been married twelve years when Asher passed away at age forty-six on November 12, 1915. Funeral services were at his home, 1003 Rio Grande, with Reverend James S. Allen, St. David's church rector, officiating.

The cause of death was apoplexy; the secondary cause was chronic malaria. Asher had been very ill for several months, but his obituary reported that although "friends feared he would not recover," he had rallied after spending some time in Colorado to rest. However, he "again became very ill and never regained strength sufficient to leave his room."

Born four years after Asher's death, his niece, Jane Smoot, wrote this impression of her uncle, drawn from family stories and her father's memories. "Daddy was like Papa. He loved the outdoors, loved the country. Uncle Asher was definitely tied to the city. He grew up with the influence of the social graces that the early years in Kentucky provided. He was highly intellectual and very comfortable in any social situation."

Following Asher's death a year after its founding, the *Austin American* newspaper continued through a series of owners and transitions, and it remains part of Austin's newspaper lexicon today. Under new ownership in 1924, the *Austin American*, the morning paper, and the *Austin Evening Statesman* merged. The Sunday edition of the *Austin American* was renamed the *Sunday*

Asher Graham Smoot, well-known Austin journalist, co-founded the *Austin American* newspaper in 1914. *Flower Hill Foundation Collection.*

American-Statesman. In 1973, the *American* and the *Statesman* combined to become an all-day newspaper issued as the *Austin American-Statesman.*

A tribute to Asher credited the journalist as being "closely identified with every progressive civic and commercial movement in Austin. He was a staunch supporter of every worthy and forward-looking cause. To him, and the *Austin American*, whose destiny he was so closely associated, this city [Austin] owes much of its municipal progress. A history of Texas journalism would be far from complete were not full mention made of Asher Graham Smoot."

The 1922 edition of *The Encyclopedia of Texas* featured Asher "A.G." Smoot. The lengthy commentary described the full scope of his work, ended with these remarks:

> *In addition to his work on these two papers, to whose interests practically his entire newspaper career was devoted, Mr. Smoot also acted from time to time as correspondent for some of the leading papers of the country, representing the Associated Press, the* New York Herald, *and other papers and associations of national importance. As a writer, Mr. Smoot gave evidence of rare ability, humor, tinged with clever analytical depiction, characterizing his style, and making his articles and editorials peculiarly readable.*

3

LAW LIBRARIAN OF
THE TEXAS SUPREME COURT

LAWRENCE KELLEY SMOOT

*L*awrence Kelley Smoot was born on August 9, 1875, in Bowling Green, Kentucky, and came to Texas with his family soon after. He was named for his mother's brother, Lawrence Graham, and his father, Richmond Kelley Smoot.

Many years later, at the request of his daughter, Lawrence wrote family stories and personal remembrances about his life. "My citizenship in Bowling Green was short. When I had just rounded out my first year it was announced that the family was moving to Austin, Texas, where my father had been elected to pastor of the First Southern Presbyterian Church."

"Flower Hill was a grand place for a small boy," Lawrence said.

> *Until I started school I had the place to myself. Papa saw to it that there was a pile of sand in the back yard all of the time. Mama always had a box full of empty spools, from which she had used the thread in making our clothes. She and I worked out a way to put those spools together and make trains of them. Those trains and that sand pile were the making of a big railroad system, with tunnels running through it. All of this was fine until our little dog would plant himself right in the middle of the entire system, thus wrecking it and I would have to rebuild.*

With his brother, Asher, who was six years older, Lawrence attended the Texas German and English Academy until the private school closed. "After Professor Bickler left Austin, to become superintendent of the public schools of Galveston, the academy closed and most of his pupils entered the public schools of Austin. I started sixth grade at West Austin Public School at West Twelfth and Rio Grande Streets." Lawrence continued in public school until the tenth grade.

By the time I reached the end of the tenth grade, after our Latin teacher married and left, the new teacher was not up to par. It didn't take me long to decide that I did not like Latin, and Algebra was another "bugaboo" that I could not get along with. Science and English were on good terms with me, but two good subjects could not pull up two bad ones, and those four constituted the curriculum.

On top of these disadvantages, my eyes went to the bad and our family doctor said the best thing for me to do was not to read any more than I had to for the next year. As school was going one way and I was going another, Papa and Mama agreed to let me drop out of school for the next few months to get my eyes well and then try it again.

After leaving school and spending all of his time at home, Lawrence developed a fascination with "all things electrical":

During all the time I had at home, I could not solve the great problem of what was my mission in this world. Going to school was not what I thought should be my life time profession, and I didn't seem to fit into anything else. At this particular time I came in contact with a former Bickler boy, who was several years my senior and who had entered the business world. His particular line was helping to install electric lights in the homes of Austin. That was a new event in Austin and many people were afraid to even cross the street where an electric wire was strung. When he came to our house [Flower Hill] I followed him all over the place—from the ground floor to the attic—helping him push wires through the partition walls, install the light fixtures, the fuse blocks and make the connections. That was it. I would be an electrical engineer, but there was another stumbling block to trip me up on the road to fame. There was no electrical school short of New York and our finances did not permit my wandering that far from home to get an electrical training, and the days of corresponding schools had not been discovered. So my first real dream of a great success in life faded away as a mirage.

Lawrence's next adventure was working at a dry goods store:

A dry goods store was a place where they sold goods to make women's dresses, supplemented by laces, ribbons, gloves, parasols, thread, table linens, stockings, sheeting and maybe purses. A year of that sort of work thoroughly convinced me, that I was not born to be a merchant. However, it made its impression in my ability to judge a good piece of cloth when it came between my fingers, in contacting people, and learning to handle small finance. The occasional trips that I made to the bank, which was in the adjoining building, put the bug in my head that a BANK was the place to make money. I have since found out that while it is where the money is, it does not necessary mean that it is the place to make money. However, the bug kept on buzzing.

The dry goods store closed, but Lawrence had saved enough money to buy his first buggy. Lawrence's eyesight had improved, and he started classes at a commercial college:

The commercial college was conducted by a man who was excellent help to those who wanted to learn, but who had little patience with those who had to be taught. Showing a disposition to learn, a number of us rapidly conquered the art of handling a cash book, the double entry ledger, and a sixteen column journal, for which we never had any use.

Professor said no one was perfect therefore he would not give a grade of 100, but he gave me a 99.9. I got my diploma and headed out into the world to be a big banker. If any in my class ever became a banker, I never heard of it. Most of them, like myself, were blocked by there being "no opening at this time."

While Lawrence was looking around for an "opening" in the banking business, the clerk of the Texas Supreme Court, who, incidentally, was his former Sunday School teacher, called and offered Lawrence an interview. As a result of that interview, the twenty-year-old became the assistant librarian of the Texas State Law Library on March 5, 1895. His salary for the first two years in this position was thirty dollars per month. Lawrence continued to live at home and wrote that this small amount helped to pay family expenses.

Never did a greener gourd grow on a gourd vine than I was in that library! A big mass of books, arranged in book cases, all looking alike and, with the exception of the numbers on their back, seemed to be exact copies of each other. My problem seemed to be, "what was it all about?" The book cases were labeled for the different states of the United States until I found in the far corner of the room a line marked "text books." I thought I had seen my last of text books when I left the school room, but here were more of them. Through a process of discovery, it began to dawn upon me what a law book was and why there were so many of them. New facts developed thick and fast, and during all of my years' work in the library I found that there was something new to be learned each day, which brings to mind an expression of our family physician, Dr. Granberry, that "when we get too old to learn, we die."

The staff that Lawrence served included the chief justice and two associates, the clerk of the Supreme Court and a chief deputy clerk along with lawyers, legislators and law students. His primary responsibility was to locate references in this public library as requested.

The library was not only a depository for law books used by the Court, but was a general meeting place and study room for the members of the Legislature, heads of the State Departments, lawyers attending the sessions of the appellate courts in Austin and law students from the University [of Texas] Law Department. At that time, the Law School was housed in the basement of the University and had practically no library of its own, but the students used the Supreme Court Library for their reference reading....By mingling with all this mass of humanity, which consisted in various degrees and types, I became acquainted not only with the local bar and judges but with the leading lawyers of that day and with the youth which were to become the leaders later on. The lawyers using the library were not aware of my slight acquaintance with the legal lore and asked many questions that, at the time, was just simply Greek to me. Their questions and their conversation impressed me with the fact that any one who conscientiously tried to handle a law library and become a walking encyclopedia for its patrons must have some knowledge of the subject, or not be worth his salt.

During his first year in the Supreme Court library, Lawrence learned that the university offered night law classes organized into a three-year

Lawrence Smoot served as an official with the Texas Supreme Court of Texas, first as librarian and then as the court reporter. He is pictured here on the steps of the Texas Capitol building in 1915. *Flower Hill Foundation Collection.*

program. He registered for this program in September 1896 with twenty-nine other young men. At the end of three years, seven received their diploma. Lawrence earned a law degree and a license as an attorney; however, it was never his intention to practice law, and he continued with his responsibilities in the library.

> *The various legislators, like most every thing else in the world, are of various kinds. Some expect to turn the world over, draft a new constitution, rearrange the entire make up of the governmental system. Some want to investigate every thing from the basement to the top of the dome, while others endeavor to correct the misdeeds of their predecessors and attend to necessary business. One of these Legislatures, the 30th [January 8, 1907–April 12, 1907] was composed of hardworking men and they certainly did start off with a bang!*
>
> *After getting organized and introducing all the bills they could think of, they took a crack at the Library, by deciding they wanted it to stay open at night* [during the legislative session], *regardless of the fact that I told them there were no lights in the library room. But, like in the prayer meeting when the minister quoted the passage that said there will "be wailing and gnashing of teeth," an old lady spoke up that she had no teeth and the minister promptly replied, "Madam, teeth will be provided," the legislators told me lights would be provided. And they were, with the result that for about four months, I spent practically all of my time from 8 a.m. to 11 p.m., including Sundays, in the library. That was a busy four months and the books in the library were in constant use. This, on top of my regular work, made me almost forget to eat, and although I was renumerated for the extra time and work, it did me no good. A few days after the Legislature adjourned, I was attacked by what I thought was appendicitis, but it developed into a case of high acidity and a general upside digestive system, which incapacitated me for the next 12 months.*

In the following years, through many changes in personnel and personalities in the leadership of the Texas Supreme Court, Lawrence continued in his responsibilities in the library. His salary was increased to sixty dollars his third year of service, and it remained so until 1907, when Lawrence's salary was increased to seventy-five dollars per month.

> *I continued to grow in the library spirit and new books coming in constantly added to the growth and usefulness of the library....During*

all the years in which so many changes were taking place, I was wrestling with the ever-growing library that was constantly being shifted from shelf to shelf in order to keep the continuing serial numbers in proper order, and, as the Court's marshal, every Wednesday attending a meeting of the Supreme Court to announce that they are in session or that they are adjourning to a future day....Mr. W.M. Harris, of the [Texas] Attorney General's Department, who had just completed an annotation of the Texas Constitution, in 1914 produced for the Bar a small pocket-sized book titled Harris' Rules of the Courts, *based on an index I had produced to help locate rules appropriate to a certain occasion. In 1922, in response to requests for an update of this work, I took over the job and produced a new edition. The demand for something better began to grow and in 1932, with the Vernon Law Book Company as the publisher, I brought forth a third effort of the rules, which was much larger and more complete than previous editions, and which contained not only the rules and their annotations, but corresponding statutes.*

Soon after completing thirty-seven years as librarian for the Texas Supreme Court, in 1932, Lawrence was promoted to the position of reporter of the court. His salary fluctuated between $250 and $316 per month, depending on the inclination of the legislature.

Described as "a sober man of regular habits" by a nephew, it appears that Lawrence's thoughtful temperament was well suited to this job. According to Texas Supreme Court history, the library under Mr. Smoot's responsibility had been mostly untouched by legislative oversight since the late 1800s, without any sizeable infusions of money until the 1950s. The day-to-day operations were in the capable hands of Lawrence Smoot. Before his hiring, there was a "lackadaisical attitude towards library resources. Books were piled on the ground, spilling into disorderly heaps."

At the time of his retirement in 1961, Lawrence had worked for the State of Texas sixty-six years, earning him the distinction as the longest tenure of state employment, a

After sixty-six years of service with the Texas Supreme Court, Lawrence Smoot retired. Photograph taken for the *Austin American-Statesman. Flower Hill Foundation Collection.*

record he held until 1989, when Gertrude LaNelle Hays retired with sixty-eight years of service to the State of Texas.

When Lawrence was interviewed for an article in the *Austin American-Statesman* about his retirement at age eighty-six, he was asked what he would do with his time now that he wouldn't be working:

> *"In other words, I'm going to retire—quit." Then he adds, in a philosophical vein that has guided his work as official court reporter for the Texas Supreme Court, "Of course, that will be up to my Maker. If he has something else for me to do, I will do it." His long years of reviewing and digesting court opinions have convinced Smoot that "outside of modern improvements" the troubles Texans now have are about like the troubles that have plagued them from the beginning.*
>
> *At the turn of the century Lawrence became marshal of the court: "it was about the same as a bailiff's job, except that during those days we sometimes had to do a little sheriffing [sic] when someone got out of line during their arguments before the court."*

For many years after Lawrence began his career at the Supreme Court library and Asher's journalism career flourished, Flower Hill continued to be home for the immediate Smoot family. The extended family was always welcome for a short visit or to stay as long as needed, and the home was an extension of Reverend Smoot's ministry. Lawrence remembered parishioners often stopping by for spiritual advice and often seeking financial assistance.

Lawrence was very much involved in the church from a young age and became a First Southern Presbyterian Church member when he was sixteen years old. He was installed to serve as a deacon at that church in 1905, served as a ruling elder beginning in 1919 and was Sabbath School superintendent for many years. "Having been born practically in the church, I suppose it was only natural that I spent a large portion of my time in the church, especially as long as Papa was the preacher. I took part in every line of the work, except preaching, from making fires in the furnace during the winter, repairing the electric lights, painting a new Sunday School room, teaching a class of boys, and ushering in the church on Sundays."

A creative man who enjoyed working with his hands, Lawrence pursued several hobbies and continued to be interested in electricity. "My liking for electricity still lingers in my blood. At the expense of a few burnt fingers and having a screwdriver knocked out of my hand, I still like to tinker with anything electrical."

(*Left to right*) Logan King, Roy Deen and Lawrence Smoot listening to an early phonograph through rubber tubes. *Flower Hill Foundation Collection.*

"Daddy had considerable talent, really artistic talent in doing woodwork, or in many other things around the home," Lawrence's daughter, Jane, explained in a 1992 interview. "Daddy designed a cistern located north of the house to catch rainwater." His design allowed for the redirection of water out toward Pressler Street if the cistern was too full. The cistern was the size of a room. The cap was removed twice a year, the cistern was drained and two men would climb down inside to clean the sides and bottom with coarse bristle brushes. "Even in his late eighties, Daddy did most of our repair work, plumbing and electrical—anything else that needed to be done. This was a true release from the academic, the legal work that he had spent so many years doing."

An intricate walnut riverboat, still displayed in the wedding parlor, is considered Lawrence's masterpiece. "He made the boat on a scroll saw that was bought for Uncle Asher when he was about ten or twelve," Jane said. "Grandfather thought it would be an ideal toy and hobby for Uncle Asher. But it turned out that he just was not interested in such things. The scroll saw sat unused for some time until Daddy became curious about it. He did have the talent and the interest. He made many, many objects on that saw. There are a number in the house and he gave away a great many of the pieces." Lawrence used the standing foot-powered scroll saw throughout his life. It still stands in the kitchen at Flower Hill.

His daughter, Jane, years later, proudly described her father's skill with wood and a saw, among other tools, to build a chicken house on the property. "Daddy made small things such as toys and wagons for me, but he not only designed the chicken house, he built it every bit, he had no help. It has a concrete floor, slanted deliberately, so when you used water to wash it off, it would drain naturally. The roof, north and west wall are corrugated iron, to protect the chickens from the cold northwest wind. He made the roosts of wood so as to make it good on the chicken's feet, because iron would freeze to them in the winter." The chickens who inhabited this fine chicken house were not ordinary chickens. "These were birds that were developed for their breast meat. The rest of the body was not anything to brag about, but the meat of the breast of those Indian Game chickens was really excellent." No doubt the bounty of these chickens often provided Smoot family meals; however, Lawrence also developed a small mail order business, shipping Indian Game chickens throughout the country.

Intricate riverboat designed and made by Lawrence Kelley Smoot on a foot-powered scroll saw. *Flower Hill Foundation Collection.*

Opposite: Jane Smoot and her father, Lawrence, with a homemade wheelbarrow on the Flower Hill driveway. *Flower Hill Foundation Collection.*

Above: Jane Smoot is helping feed the chickens near the chicken run at Flower Hill. The Smoots had a mail-order chicken business in the 1920s. *Flower Hill Foundation Collection.*

Jane remembered an experience her father had with another hobby, his sulky and horses. "He took his sulky and the horses he was training to race out to Hyde Park where there was, in the early days, a race track. At that time Hyde Park was not in the city and the track was available to time your horses. Once when Daddy had his horses at the track, a very inquisitive neighbor came out to watch him. That neighbor was none other than Elizabeth Ney! Her place was very near the track and she loved horses, too. She was very friendly and she and Daddy had many visits together." Lawrence was also an accomplished photographer, and many vintage photos in the Flower Hill archives were taken, and the film developed, by him.

As a young man, Lawrence enjoyed social outings to area lakes, including Lake McDonald and Bull Creek. One favorite outing was "Camp Pajama" held annually on the east bank of the Colorado River, near Kingsland in Burnet County. The 1903 summer camp, attended by families and single young adults, was described in the *Statesman*:

> *The enjoyment of the camp consists in good eating, fine bathing in the Colorado, and sleeping in tents with open exposure to mountain air that*

On the summit of Enchanted Rock for a sunrise sermon in 1907. Lawrence Smoot (*seated in front*) took the picture using a remote shutter and a camera set on a tripod. *Flower Hill Foundation Collection.*

> *makes a couple of blankets comfortable at night. Those coming* [to the camp] *should provide themselves with bathing suits. The camp is presided over and catered for by Mrs. Alsworth, noted as the proprietress of the Morris building, north of the capitol. Guests are all in robust health and enormous appetites. The quantity of provender stored away by even delicate women is surprising. There is plenty of tent and table room for weary mortals.*

After the death of his mother in 1916, followed by the death of Uncle Lawrence a year later and the relocation of Cousin Lena, Lawrence was, for the first time in his life, living alone. However, this quiet time at Flower Hill would not last for long.

Lawrence Kelley Smoot and Julia Emma Williams of Maysfield (near Cameron, Texas) were married in June 1918 and, according to the newspaper announcement of the event, "motored to Austin directly after their marriage" to begin their life together at Flower Hill.

In a personal essay, Lawrence describes their meeting at the Southern Presbyterian Church:

> *At church I usually went with the crowd, giving little thought to any individual, until one Sunday morning, as I was coming up the aisle from seating visitors, I saw a beautiful, auburn-haired young lady come in the*

door and down the aisle on the other side of the church auditorium. From that moment I had a desire to forsake the crowd and be alone with that young lady, even though I did not know her. I inquired as to her identity but no one knew her. After the service I saw her speak to a person I knew. I immediately asked for her name and address, and on the way home asked Papa if he knew her. He said he did not but he must have made a mental note of her name and address, because, during the following week, in his quiet way, he called upon the young lady and got her promise to come to Sunday School the next Sunday.

And, again in his quiet way, Papa asked me the next Sunday morning to go to the post office to mail a letter that he was anxious to get off. This was his good excuse to get me to go somewhere while he went on to Sunday School. When I walked into the Sunday School room, I saw the reason why. There Papa stood talking to the young lady in question. He introduced us, our eyes met, then we shook hands. From that day forward her desires have been my wishes. There have been rough roads and rocky places, but they were only temporary and the road soon became a smooth highway again.

The couple dated seventeen years before marrying. Their only child, Jane, explained in an interview,

I know this sounds fantastic to modern people but they did indeed consider themselves fully, absolutely engaged to be married. But, they had thought it out very carefully. Mother was teaching in far West Texas, which she thoroughly enjoyed. Grandfather had died and Grandmother Smoot was still living—not in good health, but she was living. Daddy took a very wise viewpoint, I think, that he would not leave this home. He would not leave Grandmother alone. And, he did not want to bring his bride into his mother's home. He did not feel that two women would one hundred percent share the home, even though Mother and Grandmother got along beautifully. Daddy knew that when he married he wanted Flower Hill to be entirely his wife's home. Somehow Mother understood this and she agreed. It seemed to be the very happy solution for all of them.

The groom advised his future bride not to bring any furniture from her family home in Milam County, as his family's furnishings filled their future home. Julia's sisters sent the Williams family crystal and china instead.

Julia received her higher education at Staunton Hall in Natchez, Mississippi, and taught in rural West Texas schools. Her teaching career spanned thirty-five years, including, after she and Lawrence married, when she taught history at John T. Allan High School and Stephen F. Austin High School in Austin. "Mother was ahead of her time using inventive projects and methods with her students," Jane said. "Her example made an impression on my teaching habits once I was in the classroom."

"Although a devoted teacher, Mother was interested in many other things in life besides books and teaching," Jane said. "She was a very high-spirited person and very ingenious in practically everything she touched. She was also very hard working, very industrious."

Julia Williams Smoot taught history in Central and West Texas for thirty-five years. *Flower Hill Foundation Collection.*

In the early 1900s, all-male Harvard University offered summer sessions for young ladies who could present "proper credentials." Jane remembers her mother saying how badly she wanted to attend this session, but Amelia, her sister, who was in charge, refused to allow it:

> *Sister was horrified that mother wanted to travel alone to attend a man's university. She also presented the fact that they didn't have the money. So, mother let it go until the next year when the same offer was made for a summer session at Harvard. She had been shrewdly saving money all year and she went to Sister and said, "I'm not asking you this time. I'm telling you that I'm going to Harvard. I have saved the money and I will do my best not to cause you, or the family, any trouble about it, but I'm going." Sister responded that she couldn't have Mother going off by herself so she would go with her.*

The sisters found a boardinghouse close to Harvard and settled in for the summer. "Well, Sister was absolutely enchanted. Harvard to her was heaven on earth. Mother certainly liked it too, but every weekend she elected to go on some kind of tour around New England while Sister was ensconced in the library. They did have a wonderful time although back home in Milam County, the idea of those two girls going off like that was as shocking as if they had gone to the moon."

The adventure didn't end when Julia and Amelia completed the summer program. The young women decided to forego a train ride home and instead booked passage on the Mallory Line steamship *Algonquin*. "They had a great trip home, docked in Galveston and then made their way back to Milam County."

"During the Depression years, Mother had to leave her teaching job at Austin High," Jane said in an oral history interview. "A rider to an appropriations bill passed by the Texas legislature declared that husband and wife could not both receive state funds." Because Austin schools received some money from the state, Julia in her teaching position and Lawrence as librarian of the Texas Supreme Court were both receiving state funds.

> *They could not both continue in these jobs. Mother got the pink slip with her May check at the end of the school year. Of course, it was only natural for Mother to give up her job instead of Daddy, but it hurt her terribly. She loved home intensely, and all of us, of course, but she was not content to spend her hours cooking and cleaning day after day. She had too much spirit to do all sorts of things and so I think, in fact I know, that this situation led her to decide that she would take over her land in Milam County.*

Julia's family owned farmland in Milam County, one hundred miles northeast of Austin. The Williams sisters—Amelia, Julia, Carrie, Hattie and Tucky—inherited the land, and for some time, it was overseen by Julia's brother-in-law Hubert Atkinson. However, after some controversy and a bit of family drama, Julia chose to manage her portion with the help of a foreman who lived on the farm. "Mother loved the land, and Daddy did too. Daddy often quoted that old saying, 'civilization begins and ends with the plow,'" Jane said. "Mother felt a deep kinship to the land as if it produced the very essence of her being. It was amazing to me that at one hundred miles distance and being on the place only on Saturday, she could accomplish as much as she did. From 1935 to 1958, only being there on Saturdays, on the whole, she had more profitable years than losing years [with the cotton crop]."

This harmony with the land made Julia well suited to carry on the cultivation and care of the grounds of Flower Hill that had begun with the ardent work of Sallie Smoot. Jane described the estate as being in a state of roughness, with her grandmother taming it into a civilized form. "My mother carried on Grandmother Smoot's plan of gardening. She kept the flowers going in the garden and around the house. All of the areas out in the

The Williams sisters in Milam County (*left to right*): Julia Williams Smoot, Amelia Worthington Williams, Carrie Williams Peets, Harriett Williams Atkinson, Virginia Williams Freeman. *Flower Hill Foundation Collection.*

yard space today that are bordered by rocks all were flower beds and were kept up beautifully."

Julia was also known for her cooking skills. "She seemed to have a natural talent because she created recipes," Jane said. "She would read a recipe and start out following it, but on the way she either had too much of one thing or not enough of something else and she would add another item that she thought would be good. By the time she was done, whatever she was preparing was quite different from the original recipe, but we always enjoyed it." Julia did not pass her cooking skills on to her daughter. Even when an older Miss Smoot lived alone at Flower Hill, John Plyler recalled that she didn't cook but loved to go out to eat.

Julia was also creative in making embroidered dresses for Jane, tatting and doing lacework on handkerchiefs and knitting. "When she was growing up it was quite the fashion for young ladies to learn how to burn wood objects for decoration, and Mother was very good at that. We still have some of her decorative boxes and bowls. The point was to trace a design on wooden pieces and then with certain awls and little burning rods, burn in the designs. The piece would be finished with some sort of varnish or wax."

During the years after Lawrence and Julia married, Flower Hill became a temporary home to many students who came to Austin to attend The University of Texas. Some of these were students that Julia had taught in rural West Texas schools when they were young. Their parents were pleased to have their daughters and sons live with the Smoots at Flower Hill rather than in a dormitory. Accommodations were made for this makeshift boardinghouse by adding sleeping porches—one on the south upstairs for the girls and another on the north upstairs for the boys. Various family members who were attending the university also lived at Flower Hill. Most paid for these accommodations, and this income helped maintain Flower Hill, especially during the depression years. "We had a variegated social situation here. The house was just jam packed full," Jane remembered in an interview in 1980. "They all slept and ate here."

Julia's natural bent toward teaching flowed into the family's home life and that of the students who were boarding at Flower Hill. "In a sense, she taught the students who lived with us just as she taught students in the classroom," Jane said. "She felt a responsibility to provide a safe place to live as well as teach proper values."

The students who boarded were expected to live under Julia's exact rules of conduct. Failure to do so could lead to punishment.

> *I early witnessed what happened to large, tall folks who somehow went astray: that is, did not come home on time; let their grades fall; did not keep their rooms orderly; or wasted food. Practical jokes were out of bounds. Julia did not respond kindly when a bucketful of live frogs was dumped onto the girls' sleeping porch. Usually delinquents received a stern talking to but occasionally parents were called and the guilty party would have to confess the misdeed and ask what the parents wanted done in response.*

Amid Julia Smoot's efficiency in supervising the household at Flower Hill, she also possessed a soft, nurturing side. When times were especially tough, she would interject humor or direct attention to an enjoyable activity. When her older sister was weary from contending with a long illness, Julia walked into Amelia's hospital room wearing an old farm hat decorated with turkey feathers. Jane remembered the unexpected, ridiculous sight that brought a smile to her Aunt Amelia's face for the first time in days. Julia used many "sayings" to teach a principle or remind someone of priorities, but one, in particular, seems to be the heart of her philosophy of life: "People before things."

Julia possessed a strong sense of how to meet the needs of others. Her student boarders needed structure; her daughter needed love, security and to learn lessons that would see her through life.

Julia Williams Smoot and
her daughter, Jane, riding in
a handmade wheelbarrow
on the Flower Hill driveway.
Flower Hill Foundation Collection.

In addition to functional structural changes after Lawrence and Julia were
married, Julia set about to add her sense of style to Flower Hill.

In an oral history recording, Jane Smoot explained how her mother was
determined to replace the slender, wooden supports on the front porch of
the house at Flower Hill. "In 1925, Mother decided, and Daddy agreed
although he didn't particularly care, that the house ought to have tall,
substantial columns. There was a large impressive old home of the Swisher
family on Fourth Street that had been vacant many years and had gone to
rack and ruin…but it had been a handsome house and it had columns that
were still in good condition."

Julia and Lawrence made arrangements with the old house owners to purchase the columns, set a price and agreed that when the front porch at Flower Hill was ready, they would arrange to move the columns. "However, in the meantime, while they were working on the front porch to get it ready, Dr. Z.T. Scott arrived in town, and he decided he liked the whole [Swisher] house, not just the columns…and he bought the whole thing, and moved it out on the lake. Of course, there were changes made, but those columns are the ones we thought were going to come to Flower Hill.

"Well, Mother, being of her nature was greatly distressed and angry clear through, clear through. She said, 'Those people promised and they went back on their word.' Daddy was somewhat quieter in nature and always philosophical, because that was the only way he knew how to live life."

Lawrence believed that sometimes things like this happen. It wasn't good that someone had reneged on their promise, but Jane remembered that her father stated, "Sometimes it does happen. We've lived this long without columns we can go on living the rest of our days without columns." But, Mother said, "No we're going to have columns!"

Julia and the building contractor working on the improved front porch set out to find a way to get the columns she so desperately wanted. "They went up the river, past Deep Eddy, where they found six enormous cypress trees. Great big ones, straight as could be. From the property owner they bought those six cypress trees, chopped off all the limbs and hauled them in here [Flower Hill]. I remember very well when that was done. And I don't know why they didn't take pictures because that was a really major undertaking."

Six cypress trees embedded in cement replaced the original porch supports. Next, the trees were bricked "around and around and around, being laid as a brick wall would be with mortar, two circles of brick. Then the outside of the brick circle was mortared, plastered over, covered in stucco and then painted." Julia had her columns. Jane added, "They don't look like Corinthian or Ionian or any of those classic designs but I have been told by architects that, structurally, they are stronger than any of the very beautiful wooden columns. And Mother was satisfied. That just shows that she did have an ability when one road closed to find another and open it up!"

Initially, the house had no closets or bathrooms. Jane explained, "That is not because we were more primitive than other people. It is just that that is how all of the houses of the time were designed. People used wardrobes or chiffoniers for their clothes and had no need for a closet. The house does now have closets, all of which my father built through the years.

"The first toilet, the only toilet, was this tiny little room wedged in the downstairs back hall, which is now a utility closet. The current, downstairs bathroom was originally part of a porch and the one upstairs was sectioned off from the front hall." Before there were bathtubs, all of the bedrooms had washstands. "Each bedroom had large bowls with matching pitchers that would hold eight to ten gallons of water at best. You would pour a bit of water into the bowl and, using a wash cloth and soap you would take what we would call a sponge bath. There would be a jar to hold the soapy water, you would refill the bowl with clean water and rinse." The first bathtubs were very small and made of galvanized tin. Eventually, in an indirect way, Austin's first porcelain tub made its way to the downstairs bathroom at Flower Hill.

"A very wealthy lumberman and Mayor of Austin from 1887 to 1889, Captain Nalle, who bought property east of Flower Hill, shipped a porcelain tub from New York to Galveston and then arranged to bring it to Austin via train. This was in the early 1890s and that tub was the marvel of the town. Years later when that place was torn down, no one wanted the old tub and it was cast aside. However, Mother wanted it and insisted on buying it." Nalle's son, Ernest, was the brother-in-law of Asher Smoot, and because of this connection and because Ernest was eager to get rid of the tub, he offered to give it to Julia. "But Mother couldn't take it without paying something for it. Finally, he told her to give him a dollar for each man it took to lift it. Only ten men could fit around the tub and even then, it was a strain to lift. Mother said it was just unthinkable to give only ten dollars for the tub, so she paid twenty dollars for it. That tub was quite an uplift in the world of personal cleansing at Flower Hill!"

Monday was laundry day, and young Jane enjoyed playing among the iron washpots set up under the trees behind the house. Flower Hill pets—dogs and cats—were always present to keep Jane company. "We didn't have a washing machine until after World War II. We used large pots set up outside....One of the pots sat on bricks and a fire was built underneath," Jane explained:

> That pot had boiling water, just like Shakespeare's cauldron, and the other would have cold water [for rinsing]. We used lye soap that we made. It didn't have the fragrance of modern soaps, but it really got the clothes clean. Of course, somewhere along, if the clothes were dirty enough there had to be a rubbing board to rub by hand to get them really clean....The clothes were rung out by hand and placed on a large board to

The Smoots kept a number of beloved pets over the years. Here is Jane Smoot on the grounds of Flower Hill with her black cat. *Flower Hill Foundation Collection.*

Another dearly loved Flower Hill pet sits perched atop a fence with Jane Smoot. *Flower Hill Foundation Collection.*

carry to the lines where they were hung to dry. The clothes would flap and blow and, as a young child, that was interesting to me to watch. Later in the day, we took the dry clothes off the lines and then, guess who had to iron? Mother hated ironing so as soon as I was tall enough to safely reach the ironing board, she taught me how to iron.

I remember when Calcasieu Lumber Company put an advertisement in the paper that they were taking a list of people who wanted to buy a Bendix washing machine. The machines wouldn't be in stock for a while, but this was right at the end of the Second World War and they would sell the machines in the order as people signed up. I couldn't wait to get down there *and I was number fourteen to sign up. In the fall of 1981 the washing machine was still doing just fine. I was about to go on a wonderful trip to Africa. Before I left I knew the Bendix was leaking, but it wasn't leaking very much and I was busy. I thought that no one would use it while I was gone and I could wait and have it fixed when I got back home. That's where I made a mistake. I was gone for more than a month and, during that time it kept leaking. By the time I returned, the whole motor had rusted. I was reminded of what I'd been brought up on, and yet I had not followed it: a stitch in time saves nine.*

Early-day Flower Hill would be considered an urban farm today, as productive as a rural farm, but on a smaller scale. The care of the animals was primarily the responsibility of Willis Maxwell, the African American man who lived in the lumber room behind the house. "Maxwell was part cook and helped in the house, but he also helped with yard work. He was a general handy man and very much a part of our everyday life," Jane said. In a notebook titled "I Remember," Jane wrote about the fond memory of "Jule" (her name for Jenny Moore, who also worked for the Smoot family) and Maxwell playing with her by the fireplace in the library. She also remembered a "very heavy snowstorm when Jule caught a freezing red bird out by the side door and caged it for me." Sadly, another memory Jane wrote was "finding Maxwell dead in the kitchen one cold winter morning when I was about eight years old. Even now I can feel the horror that enveloped me as I looked at the twisted body there on the floor by the sink, a biscuit pan still clutched in one hand, and biscuits scattered all over the floor."

"The care of the grounds was a secondary responsibility to everyone who lived here," Jane explained.

The university students who were boarding with us were busy and the place was just like an anthill with people. There was so much going on! We maintained two vegetable gardens that I remember from my childhood. Each of us in the family had a part of the yard we were to take care of. The students were expected to pitch in. At the time it was so usual and routine that I didn't think about it, but I realize now that we all worked physically very hard. We allowed the lawn areas to grow naturally and those were not mowed for many years. The horses did that job. We bought our first lawn mower in the 1920s. That was Daddy's plaything!

Willis Maxwell on the path near the north garden at Flower Hill. *Flower Hill Foundation Collection.*

Bundled up, Jane Smoot enjoys a rare Austin snowfall in the 1920s. *Flower Hill Foundation Collection.*

Lawrence and Julia enjoyed forty-five years of marriage until her death in 1963. As demonstrated by letters and notes he wrote to his wife, Lawrence was a devoted husband. On the couple's fifteenth wedding anniversary in 1933, he wrote:

> *My Own Dear Julia, As each year goes by I find myself more in love with you than ever, in fact I am getting so I do not want to leave you, but wish to be by your side at all times.*
>
> *May the coming years be the happiest you have ever spent and may each one bring you a greater blessing than the preceding ones.*
>
> *Hoping that we may have many happy years together and with our own dear little Jane. I am always your devoted Lawrence.*

To maintain an emotional connection between Julia and her family, Jane commissioned a tall granite monument and installed it in the Williams

My own dear Julia:

Thirty two years ago today I gave my hand to the girl who was to rule the destiny of my future happiness, and the moment I clasp your hand in mine I realized that I had met my mate for life.

And as I realized on that morning, that you were the one girl on earth that I love, I say to you now that you still the one girl that I love - always have loved and always will love, only a hundred times more. May we both live to enjoy this love for many, many years,

Your devoted
Lawrence.

Feby 23, 1933.

Love letter from Lawrence Smoot to his wife, Julia, February 23, 1933. *Flower Hill Foundation Collection.*

family plot of the Little River Cemetery in Milam County. However, Julia is buried in the Smoot family plot at the Oakwood Cemetery in Austin.

Jane enjoyed a close relationship with her father that grew even stronger after the death of her mother. One subtle indication of the importance of this relationship to Jane is her retention for many years after her father's death of the personalized auto license plates—LKS—that her father had used on his cars. For several years, the renewal of his personalized license plates was Jane's annual birthday gift to her father. "A gift he can enjoy all year."

Above: Three Williams sisters pictured by a twenty-foot wall of blooming jasmine at Flower Hill. *Flower Hill Foundation Collection.*

Left: West Sixth Street was renumbered multiple times over the years while the Smoot family lived at Flower Hill. Lawrence Smoot hangs the new street number sign on a tree near the street. *Flower Hill Foundation Collection.*

Father and daughter took trips together, and Lawrence escorted Jane to many Austin social events. When he was ninety-one, after a thorough physical examination by a physician, Jane and Lawrence traveled to Europe for the first time. "Daddy enjoyed life right to the very last. We planned the trip so that he could have some part of every day to rest and I was the one who was glad when rest time came," Jane said. 'He got around all over those castles and every place. In fact, at 3:00 in the morning, we were going down the Champs Elysees in Paris after having been to the Folies Bergère. He enjoyed that, too."

Lawrence Smoot died at home on June 29, 1968, at age ninety-two. His only survivor was his daughter, Jane.

4

DISTINGUISHED TEXAS SCHOLAR
AND HISTORIAN

DR. AMELIA WORTHINGTON WILLIAMS

*J*ulia Smoot's sister Amelia was born on March 25, 1876, in Milam County, Texas. When Amelia was twenty-two years old, her parents died, leaving her with the responsibility of four younger sisters and the family's two-thousand-acre farm. "I've often thought Amelia lived an amazing life of courage," Jane Smoot, her niece, said in an interview. "I guess we all rise to do what we must do and Amelia certainly did. She was a born scholar—an academic perfectly and excellently from one inch of her to the other. It was a natural talent and genius."

Amelia's early education was schooling from a local minister. Still, as an indication of her natural intelligence, she was accepted to Ward Belmont, a prestigious finishing school for young ladies in Nashville, Tennessee, for further education.

Soon after Amelia returned home from Ward Belmont, her widowed mother, Emily Massengale, died, leaving Amelia with the responsibility of her sisters and the family farm. "I can imagine this was difficult for her," Jane said. "She was just ready to go out into the world and make whatever she could of herself when this happened. She felt that her first dedication had to be to her little sisters." Amelia, "with the help of workers who lived and worked on the farm, had to be entirely self supporting. There was a long stretch of floods and other weather that devastated the crops, which meant no income. They had to have vegetable gardens and slaughter their own animals. It was a rough, hard time." As guardian of her sisters, Amelia ensured that they received advanced education at well-respected schools for young women.

Amelia Worthington Williams at the age of sixteen in Calvert, Texas. *Flower Hill Foundation Collection.*

When her sisters and the farm no longer needed constant oversight, Amelia attended Stuart Seminary in Austin. After passing exams for temporary certification, she taught history and English in several rural towns in West Texas. During this time, she continued to attend college during the summers. In 1922, Amelia earned an undergraduate degree at Southwest Texas State Normal School (now Texas State University) in San Marcos.

In 1925, Amelia moved to Austin to live at Flower Hill with her sister and brother-in-law, Julia and Lawrence Smoot, and their daughter, Jane. Julia felt that her older sister had sacrificed much to care for her siblings. She offered Amelia this opportunity to continue with her education without the burden of maintaining a home. Amelia, affectionately called "Sister" by family, enrolled at The University of Texas. She earned her doctorate in history in 1931 when she was fifty-five years old under the professorship of Eugene C. Barker, PhD. Her dissertation, "Critical Study of the Siege of the Alamo and the Personnel of Its Defenders," showcased her extensive primary research on the survivors of the Alamo.

Many years later, Dr. Williams's work sparked some controversy concerning its accuracy. Lonn Taylor, a longtime historian at the Smithsonian Institution's National Museum of American History and Amelia's distant cousin, included a chapter about Dr. Williams in his book *Texas People, Texas Places*:

> *It* [Dr. Williams's dissertation] *was the first scholarly study of that battle and for many years was the only source for the list of the men who*

Amelia Worthington Williams, PhD, taught history at The University of Texas from 1925 to 1951. Her dissertation was the first scholarly study of the survivors of the Alamo. *Flower Hill Foundation Collection.*

died there. In fact, Cousin Amelia provided the names of the Alamo heroes that are carved in stone on Pompeo Coppini's imposing monument on Alamo Plaza in San Antonio. Of course, no such list is ever complete, even though it is carved in stone, and other scholars have added to and even subtracted from the list of 181 defenders....I don't remember Cousin Amelia as a misrepresenter or fabricator of anything, only as a nice old lady with her silver hair in braids who was my grandmother's cousin and who gave me an inscribed copy of one of her books, Following General Sam Houston, *when I was seven.*

Taylor also quotes another historian, Todd Hansen, author of *The Alamo Reader*, an eight-hundred-page compilation of source material on the Alamo. Hansen related Amelia's research methods to Taylor:

She searched the records of the General Land office in Austin for the names of people who had been given a land grant because a husband or father had been killed at the Alamo, and then she drove a Model T Ford all over Texas persuading their descendants to look into their attics for letters, diaries, and other documents that might throw light on the battle. She tracked down and interviewed the grandchildren of Susanna Dickenson, one of the few Alamo survivors, who told her the stories about the siege that their grandmother had told them. Finally, in June 1931, she defended her dissertation and was awarded the doctorate. She was fifty-five years old. She went on to have a productive teaching and writing career at the university that lasted for twenty more years.

Many years after her death, Amelia's formidable work continues to be held in high esteem by many. The 2012–18 Texas state historian, Bill O'Neal, recently commended Dr. Williams's "brilliant research on the Alamo as an excellent resource for this critical part of our state's history."

Five chapters of Dr. Williams's dissertation were published in the *Southwestern Historical Quarterly* in 1933 and 1934. Amelia taught American and English history at The University of Texas from 1925 until her retirement in 1951.

In the twentieth century, the three women of Flower Hill—mother Julia, daughter Jane and aunt Amelia—enjoyed a close, loving relationship. However, as you might expect, strong women sharing a living space had challenging times, especially when Amelia's influence on her niece didn't meet with Julia's approval. At the end of a list of her birthday gifts recorded

Book list recorded in Jane Smoot's childhood diary along with a list of other gifts received at Christmas 1931. *Flower Hill Foundation Collection.*

Amelia Worthington Williams, PhD, served as the coeditor, alongside Dr. Eugene C. Barker, of the Sam Houston papers and was working on a biography of Sam Houston at the time of her death.

in Jane's diary in 1933 is this notation: "My birthday has come and gone. I got a pin, a dress, and a white bead purse and two hundred dollars. Mother and Sister had a fuss over it [the money gift] because Sister gave it to me." No doubt, Jane's close relationship with Sister broadened her perspective of life. At times the aunt was a best friend to the only child, other times a surrogate mother and, in some circumstances, a buffer between Jane and her mother.

In a letter to her sister Carrie, Amelia expressed some concern that twelve-year-old Jane might have been kept too close to home by her mother but conceded that "the child is not spoiled" and "is obedient and seldom talks pertly to any of us. She is perter to her daddy than to anyone else, but I think that's because he plays with her so much. She thinks he is about her age."

"History was always Sister's consuming passion, but particularly Texas history," Jane said. "She had the vision to realize that although people around here knew pretty much what had happened in the early days of the state, they didn't have a lot of documentation or records. She set out to do an exhaustive, complete study of the siege and fall of the Alamo and everything pertaining to it. She got in her little tin Henry Ford and went all around Bexar County, up and down the Texas coast—anywhere anything pertaining to Texas history had occurred." Jane emphasized that in continued writings about the Alamo, "if you look down in the fine print of the footnotes and acknowledgements, sooner or later you're going to find acknowledgement of Amelia as one of their sources. Often our conversations at the family dinner table revolved around Sister's current research findings," Jane said, "She was a champion of recording accurate, historical information."

Dr. Williams was made an honorary lifetime member of the Daughters of the Republic of Texas and was also a member of Daughters of the American Revolution, United Daughters of the Confederacy and Order of the Eastern Star. Many of her books and all of her historical collections of journals, letters, writings and notes are held at the Eugene C. Barker History Center of The University of Texas.

Jane's beloved aunt died on August 14, 1958, and is buried in the Williams family plot in the Little River Cemetery, Milam County, Texas.

5
GUARDIAN, NURSE, DEVOTED FRIEND

JENNY MOORE

*J*enny Moore was an intimate and essential part of life at Flower Hill for three generations. Like Richmond Smoot, her journey to Texas began in Tennessee; however, her circumstances were very different.

"Jenny was 15 years old when slavery was abolished and she came to Texas with a family migrating westward after the Civil War. She continued living with them in their settlement near Hornsby's Bend (east of Austin) until she heard that there was better work available in town," Jane Smoot wrote. "Jenny and my grandparents arrived in Austin at about the same time…and they needed each other. Somehow they connected and Jenny became an integral part of the Smoot household."

During the early years of Jane Smoot's life, both of her parents were working—Julia teaching and Lawrence at the Texas Supreme Court—and Jenny took care of their only child as if she were her own. Indeed, Julia depended heavily on Jenny's help when students began "boarding" at Flower Hill, significantly increasing food preparation, cleaning and laundry.

In a remembrance written in 1991, Jane described Jenny as having an "aquiline nose, flashing eyes, and ramrod straight posture. From the time I was born, she was my nurse, my guardian, my playmate, and, until her last breath decades later, she was my devoted friend."

Jenny was intelligent and resourceful, and even though she didn't learn to read or write, she was an astute businesswoman. She was widowed twice but supported her children, providing them with a secure, loving home. Realizing

Jenny Moore, pictured on the grounds of Flower Hill. *Flower Hill Foundation Collection.*

Outdoor sink on the dining porch of Flower Hill, used to wash vegetables and cut flowers from the garden and greenhouses. Photograph by J.R. Thompson, 2018. *Flower Hill Foundation Collection.*

she needed to own property to ensure a secure future for her family, Jenny selected a piece of land and set about to pay for it. During an oral history interview, Jane told Jenny's story:

> *She wanted to buy land and approached Mr. Niles Graham about some acreage he owned on the eastern boundary of what is now O. Henry Junior High School [2610 West Tenth Street]. They agreed on how much an acre Jenny would pay for the parcel of land. In order to pay for this place, because she had no money other than enough to keep her going day to day*

Jenny Moore holds two-and-a-half-month-old Jane at Flower Hill. *Flower Hill Foundation Collection.*

and month to month, she promised Mr. Graham she would pay as she was able. He was very kind to allow her all the time she needed.

For some years she carried a gunnysack, as we called burlap sacks in those days, on her back as she went through all the wood land west of Shoal Creek and north of the river picking up the bones of wild animals that had died. This may seem odd that bones of that kind would have any value, but in those days they were considered valuable. Jenny brought the bones into town, walking because she walked every place she went, and sold them to Tom Miller, who owned the Hide House located downtown. Those bones were used as fertilizer and as a source of phosphorus. Over the years, as she continued to pick up bones and sell them to Mr. Miller, she managed to pay a little more and a little more on her piece of land. Jenny eventually paid the agreed price and Mr. Graham gave her a full deed for the property.

Jenny brought up her children there and as her sons married, she built other houses on the acre of land for them. In turn, they raised their families there so, at the time she died, they had quite a little compound.

I don't know for certain when Jenny died, but I believe it was in the 1940s....She was strong to the last. A really amazing person!"

Jenny is often mentioned in Jane's childhood diaries, and in the seventh grade, Jane paid tribute to this special person in an essay titled "The Most Interesting Person I Know." The twelve-year-old described Jenny's "work-worn hands [that] are knotty and rough looking, but they can very tenderly soothe a little child's hurts. She is the best playfellow I ever had; she knows exactly all the best games to play, and she can tell wonderful stories of little children in slavery times. She can make a child mind, too, but is never mean or cross."

Jenny Moore was a true line that reached directly from Richmond and Sallie Smoot through three generations to their granddaughter, Jane. Although we don't know Jenny's exact birth date, she was most likely in her late twenties when Lawrence Smoot was born in 1875 and her early seventies when Jane Smoot was born in 1919. Jenny Moore lived past ninety years old and died in the mid-1940s. She warrants a place in history as one of the strong women of Flower Hill alongside Sallie, Julia, Amelia and Jane.

6

EXEMPLARY EDUCATOR WITH WANDERING FEET

MISS JANE SMOOT

*M*iss Jane Smoot, the third-generation Smoot to live at Flower Hill, often expressed the opinion that her life was ordinary and routine, but her family—her grandparents, her parents and her Aunt Amelia—was worthy of a place in history. Jane spent much of her time and energy ensuring this would happen.

However, her dedication to the preservation of her family's legacy is only part of her story. Jane was a respected English teacher in the Austin public school system for a little over forty years, touching the lives of thousands of students in a positive, meaningful way. She was loved by many, and although her high standards might be challenging to meet, students knew they would have Miss Smoot's unwavering support.

Jane was born on December 13, 1919, to Lawrence and Julia Smoot. She was named for her paternal grandmother, Sarah Jane Smoot. Her father delighted in the birth of his only child. In a personal essay, he wrote: "As a result of my meeting Julia in that Sunday School room a golden-haired young lady has come into our family circle. She has given both of us many joys and much happiness, and my sincere prayer is that we three may walk in the light of our Savior for many years and until He sees proper to call us to a higher home, where the trials of this world will be of no consequence."

A precocious child, Jane started kindergarten in Sutton Hall on the UT campus when she was four years old and enrolled at Mathews Elementary the following year. "My participation in kindergarten was in a program at the University of Texas organized to analyze the possible kindergarten

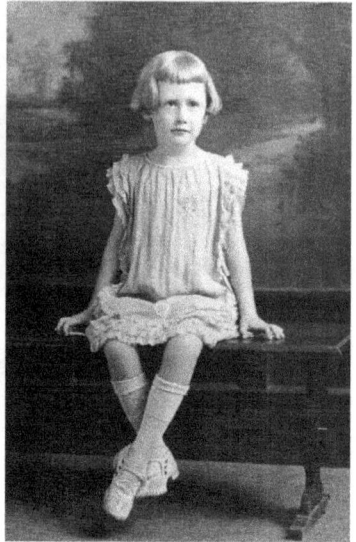

Left: Jane Smoot on the grounds of Flower Hill, 1920s. *Flower Hill Foundation Collection.*

Right: A studio portrait of Jane Smoot, five years old. *Flower Hill Foundation Collection.*

experience. I suppose I was sort of a guinea pig. This was a new concept for Austin and my mother was very interested to find out what this kindergarten business was like."

In 1928, Jane was in the fourth grade at Mathews Elementary, and one of her short compositions (with a surprise ending), titled, "My Corncob Doll," was published in the *Austin American-Statesman*: "In the summer, just after school had closed, I did not know what to do one day, so Mother told me to go and make some corn cob dolls, like she used to make when she was a little girl. So I did. Some of them looked so funny and I burned them up."

After beginning junior high school at John T. Allen Junior High School, the young girl attended summer school every year, taking as many courses as she could during that time. Jane started at The University of Texas at age fifteen and began her teaching career before her twentieth birthday. Her major at UT was British and American literature with additional special studies in French, German and education.

After the marriage of Lawrence and Julia, life at Flower Hill became more structured. The late-night impromptu weddings and garden parties of the previous generation were only a memory. "So from the time I was very young, I didn't have, in the summer time, hours and days and weeks to do whatever a lot of other children were doing," Jane said in an interview.

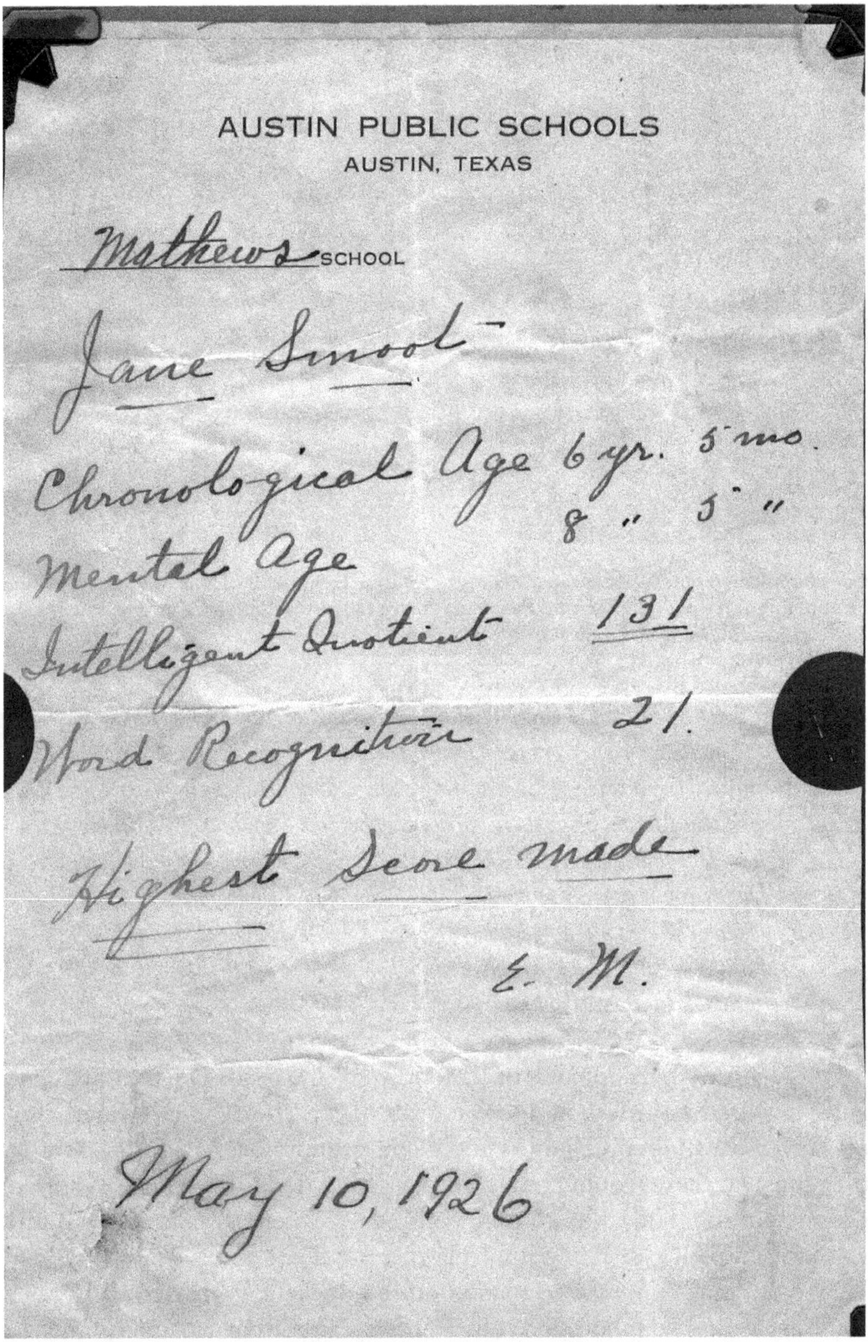

AUSTIN PUBLIC SCHOOLS
AUSTIN, TEXAS

Mathews SCHOOL

Jane Smoot -

Chronological Age 6 yr. 5 mo.

Mental Age 8 " 5 "

Intelligent Quotient _131_

Word Recognition 21.

Highest Score made

E. M.

May 10, 1926

Jane attended elementary school at Mathews Elementary School, located on West Lynn Street in Austin. This note documents her mental age and IQ score at six years, six months. *Flower Hill Foundation Collection.*

Cousins crowded onto a pedal car. (*Left to right*) Andrew Freeman Jr., Julian Freeman, Amelia Freeman, Jane Smoot and Virginia Freeman. Photographed by Lawrence Kelley Smoot, 1923. *Flower Hill Foundation Collection.*

The daily schedule at Flower Hill was structured to allow for completion of the necessary chores around the work schedule of Mother and Daddy and my school schedule. After I started to school, from seven until nine in the evening was time set aside for me to do school work. That was it. No more, no less. If I didn't have enough lessons to last the two hours, then Mother or Daddy could give me more. If I had more than I could finish in those two hours, the next morning after we got up at five, I would be excused from setting the breakfast table to finish my schoolwork. This discipline taught me the value of time.

Many times Jane looked back fondly at the years when Lawrence and Julia had boarders at Flower Hill. "I was born into a house full of university students," Jane said. "One group would come and, after they finished, here would come another group. I was a teenager before it dawned on me that I was an only child. There were so many here that I was used to plenty of company."

"We did make time for recreation on the weekends. I played with other children in the neighborhood, often family came from Milam County to visit and I enjoyed the freedom of playing in our large yard." In her diary, a young Jane wrote:

Young Jane Smoot with her doll outside a Flower Hill greenhouse. *Flower Hill Foundation Collection.*

My aunt gave me a pair of mallard ducks, which stayed in our back yard and helped keep the place free of bugs and worms. They are very interesting and exceedingly curious. No matter how cold the weather, they took a morning and evening bath in ice-cold water.

In our front yard we had two large fish ponds, one surrounded by reddish fossil rocks and the other, by grayish honey-comb rock. We had many fish in these ponds—all varieties in size, shape, and color. I would get nearly as much pleasure from the glimmering gold lights in the dark water as from the green and gray-backed ducks.

A lifelong friend of Jane, Gretchen (McElroy) Alley, provided an oral history interview in 1997 describing life on West Sixth Street in the early 1920s.

I was six years older than Jane, but we were friends and often played together at Flower Hill. And, Jane was often in our home. Before Jane started to school, my mother would keep her while Julia taught school. She taught Jane how to play the piano. Still today Jane and I are friends. I enjoy her company and we like to go out to eat. She has traveled all over the world, something I would never do. She always brings me a little gift from her trips.

Left: Portrait of Jane Smoot taken when she was fourteen years old. *Flower Hill Foundation Collection.*

Right: Austin High School graduation, 1933, Jane Smoot on the front porch of Flower Hill. *Flower Hill Foundation Collection.*

Jane wrote in her diary that she had fond memories of staying with Mrs. McElroy while "all the folks were away at work. Gretchen's paper dolls fascinated me. Mrs. McElroy's cooking was delicious!"

Jane remembered that her family was the last one in the neighborhood to have a radio and possibly the last in Austin to have a television. "Riding the streetcar was a real treat," she said. "Especially the beautiful loop all the way around Hyde Park. We would get off downtown and go to Lammes for ice cream. During warm weather, we often went to Deep Eddy to swim. Daddy believed that swimming was a necessary skill for protection of life. He always said, very seriously, that you needed to know how to swim 'in case the dam breaks.' I have fond memories of the wonderful hamburgers Daddy would buy me after we'd been swimming." The Smoots, often joined by Milam County cousins and Flower Hill boarders, would spend sunny days at Bull Creek, taking large baskets of food for a picnic. Jane remembered "the climb to the top of Mount Bonnell in our rickety old Ford and how terrified Mother was. Once we were there, the view was stunning."

In an effort to keep cool in the summer, the Smoots spent most of their time outdoors on one of the four Flower Hill porches. Jane Smoot is pictured here with one of her dolls and their matching rocking chairs. *Flower Hill Foundation Collection.*

There are many entries in Jane's diaries about the family trips to Milam County to visit Julia's family and, for many years, to oversee farmland owned by Julia. "Mother determined that she would manage her portion of land in Milam County even though it was one hundred miles away," Jane said in an oral history interview in 1992. "So, we would go up there every Saturday of the world, leaving here about four o'clock in the morning so as to get there by daybreak. Then we would leave there about ten or eleven at night or later to come back home. Nothing kept us from making these Saturday trips unless someone was very ill or there was ice [on the roads]. If someone happened to be only slightly ill that one would just stay home and the others went."

In her diary, thirteen-year-old Jane described a special Saturday with friends at Flower Hill. The entry was accompanied by her drawing of the girls and Sister preparing the meal:

Last Saturday Mother and Mrs. Palm had to superintend a hooked rug show at the Public Library. While they were there, Martha, Mary and Zolinda came over to see me. Well, we ran races, took the dogs out, swung out on the front porch, and finally went in to cook our own supper. Only it ended in Sister doing most of it. Everything was awfully good though. After

Above: Roadside picnic with baby Jane Smoot. *Flower Hill Foundation Collection.*

Left: Flower Hill horse-collar driveway in 1932. Jane Smoot, age twelve, poses with a large piece of Texas honeycomb rock. *Flower Hill Foundation Collection.*

we were through, we played games until Mother and Mrs. Palm and Daddy came back, which was real late. We had a fine time, but it's a wonder that we weren't all sick from eating so much.

After she graduated from high school in 1935, part of Jane's preparation for higher education was a college theme she wrote two months before her sixteenth birthday. The essay gives us an insight into the values and expectations of her parents and also reveals Jane's forthright manner of expressing her opinions, a characteristic that remained constant throughout her life. The essay was titled "Why I Am Going to the University and What I Expect to Get Out of It."

When asked why I am going to college and what I expect to get out of the four years spent there, I must frankly admit that I have no personal reasons for going, nor any well developed desires to be fulfilled by going. I have not yet had my sixteenth birthday, and, being neither precocious nor very ambitious, I have not even selected a vocation; nor have I thought very seriously about it.

However, my parents have had ambitions for me since the day of my birth and hopes of my success in all sorts of vocations, ranging from the author of the "great American novel" to a dentist. Having started me off in the kindergarten at the age of four, and having seen me through the Austin Public Schools from the first grade through the eleventh, it is natural that they should next present me as a victim of the faculty of the University of Texas. If my wild wishes had been considered, I would probably have packed myself off to some girls' boarding school fifteen minutes' drive from the Nation's Capital. You see, my head was full of the girlish gaiety and mischief that was the basis for the series of boarding school novels that I chanced to read. But after several applications of "sound reasoning" on the part of my parents, I blithely stepped to the firing line and accepted my gun.

The impish tone of the opening paragraphs of Jane's essay is quickly replaced by an insight that more accurately reveals maturity and the wisdom that guided her life: "The process of being educated, I think, lasts all one's life, and therefore, the years beginning with kindergarten days and ending when the student comes from the platform with his B.A. degree are merely the foundation upon which to begin real work."

Although Jane enjoyed school tremendously and continuing classes through the summer seemed natural for her, she also realized during her high school years that there was a practical reason for her to finish school early. "We were getting into the depression years and it began to look like a very good thing for me to go on and get my degree and then get out and get a job," Jane said in an oral history interview. "Mother recognized that my having a job would be a good situation; however, she wisely encouraged me to continue straight through, ensuring that I had earned my Masters. Having that degree would earn me a higher salary. And, sure enough, all the way through my teaching career I always got the top salary. I was deeply pleased and appreciative of this fact. At the end of forty years, I worked up to the maximum of $18,000 a year and I was proud of it."

The same realistic, practical attitude kept Jane in Austin for her college education. "About a year or two before graduation from high school I hoped I might go to Agnes Scott in Decatur, Georgia, just outside of Atlanta," Jane said. "It is a Presbyterian school and, at that time it was a very strong school and appealing for a number of reasons. Many of my friends in high school were going to girls' finishing schools in the East or the North—mostly in Virginia—but Agnes Scott appealed to me and I did so want to go there. But, financial matters in 1935 did not allow for any extras in the budget and no coverage for anything like going that far away to school and being maintained there. And, I knew that. I didn't have to be told. So I just stopped thinking about Agnes Scott and knew that I was very fortunate indeed to be able to live at home and go to a large, excellent university such as the University of Texas right here within walking distance of only three miles."

In keeping with a family tradition, Jane's career was in the field of education. She earned her undergraduate degree from The University of Texas in 1938 and her master's degree in 1939. Tuition was twenty-five dollars for the "long-term" semester, and the six-week summer term tuition was twelve dollars and fifty cents. Beginning immediately after earning her master's degree, she taught English and foreign languages at University Junior High School. Later she taught at Z.T. Fulmore Junior High, Stephen F. Austin High School and W.B. Travis High School.

In a personal remembrance about teaching at Fulmore, Jane recalled the view from her room on the second floor:

So far I am the only teacher to have used it [this room], *and I have experienced many ups and down within these four walls. Especially shall I remember the inspiring view from the windows—the Violet Crown of Austin lies spread before me. Those hills change moods as would a person. I have seen them smiling blue under a happy sun in a cloudless sky. And,*

I have seen the black of storm clouds boiling at a furious rate over those hills. In the early mornings soon after the day's program begins I have seen the southbound train puffing its busy way through the pass to San Antonio, Laredo, Monterey, Mexico City. Three times a day the Braniff commercial planes wing their magical way past my windows. Not to mention the swarms of Army planes that are eternally to be seen and heard. My heart reaches out to fly with them!

Jane took leave from AISD and taught English to soldiers returning from World War II at The University of Texas at Austin from 1945 to 1948. This experience with students taking advantage of the government's GI Bill to obtain an education was gratifying. "The two and a half years I taught at the University was a special joy because the students were, for the most part, serious about learning," Jane said. "It was really a tremendously happy experience." However, once this particular student population declined, the teaching staff was reduced accordingly, and Jane's teaching position was eliminated. She returned to the Austin Public School system to teach senior English and serve as Department Chair until her retirement in 1979. Miss Smoot's final twenty-six years of teaching were at Travis High School.

There was, however, a gap of time between Jane's exit from her university teaching job to reentry into the Austin Public School system. "This all happened at the beginning of the summer and there were no openings [for teachers] for the summer semesters and really no promise of anything in the fall," Jane said. "That was the summer when I decided I'd make my living by typing theses. Now, if I had been an expert typist that would have been one thing, but I wasn't. I had done a great deal of my own typing, but I was not fast, and I was just not perfect. In those days, the typist had to furnish all the paper and the university required Lancaster bond, 18-pound for theses and they required two major [original] copies with four carbons." Jane recalled putting her cards up on all of the campus bulletin boards advertising her typing service, and she was soon "loaded up" with work. "I was afraid to turn down work, for fear word would get around that I was overloaded and then I wouldn't have enough work. I needed all the work I could

For over forty years, Jane Smoot taught English with the Austin Independent School District. *Flower Hill Foundation Collection.*

possibly get to make up for not having a teaching salary." The going rate in the summer of 1948 for typing service was twenty-five cents for the original page and ten cents for each carbon copy. "This was a learning experience, too," Jane said. "I was appalled at some of the theses that I typed, yet it was none of my business to make any comments or corrections. It was torture!"

This typing endeavor did not end well. Amid Jane's heavy load of work, she was in an automobile accident that left her unable to complete the "boxes of work" she had accepted. "I had to give up the typing and I felt terrible about it because I'd promised all these people. Aunt Amelia was a God send. Bless her heart, she went around all over the campus and removed my cards from the bulletin boards and then proceeded to return each assignment to its rightful owner, with apologies."

As with every family in our country during the Great Depression and the difficult years following, the Smoots were more frugal than usual. "We had to be extremely careful, and we wasted not one thing; however, we never lacked food or clothing or heat," Jane said. "Mother made by hand most of my clothes or I wore 'hand me downs' from three of my girl cousins who were older than I that Mother would 'refashion' for me."

"We have always had a large number of books in our home," Jane said. "Back in the Depression years in the late 1920s and early 1930s, when things were pretty rough, we had a good deal of difficulty with all kinds of financial problems. It occurred to us that maybe it was senseless to keep dusting books that might bring us some cash. So, I took an armful up to Miss Fannie Ratchford, at the University, and asked her how much they would be worth and whether we could sell them. She put her arm around me and said, 'Well, now, Honey, if they have any particular value, you just take them home and put them back on the shelf. I don't think you could sell them.' So, we laughed about our valuable, historic books."

Lawrence's job with the Texas Supreme Court was secure; however, there was no guarantee his paycheck would have state money to back it. "If the state treasury didn't have enough money to meet all of the employee checks, the state would issue a list of check numbers that were not going to be covered," Jane explained. "Daddy would get his check but that didn't mean we would have money. Eventually the state would make good on these checks, but we might have to wait months."

"Holidays were very special at Flower Hill, even when money was scarce," Jane said. "When I was young I remember that every Christmas morning in Daddy's big old Underwood typewriter was a typed letter from 'Santy Claus.' Daddy always explained very seriously that Santy Claus was a little tired by the time he got here and he liked to sit down and rest a few minutes. And, while he rested, he just used the typewriter and wrote me a little letter." Lawrence made many toys for his only daughter to receive for Christmas. Perhaps the most special of these gifts is an intricate dollhouse and doll furniture still on display at Flower Hill. With electric lights and wallpaper that matched the walls of Flower Hill, the custom-made, two-story house provided Jane with hours of entertainment.

The Smoots celebrated Thanksgiving with a traditional large meal shared with relatives and friends; however, football also played a big part in this holiday. "My folks, to my surprise, were very, very excited about football. The competition between the University and A&M was a big, big thing. Along with the game in Austin every other year, there was a big parade downtown."

New Year's Eve was treated with a certain reverence, the family considering it a conscious symbol of a new beginning. "We all waited up

The Flower Hill dollhouse made by Lawrence Smoot was a Christmas gift to his daughter, Jane. *Flower Hill Foundation Collection.*

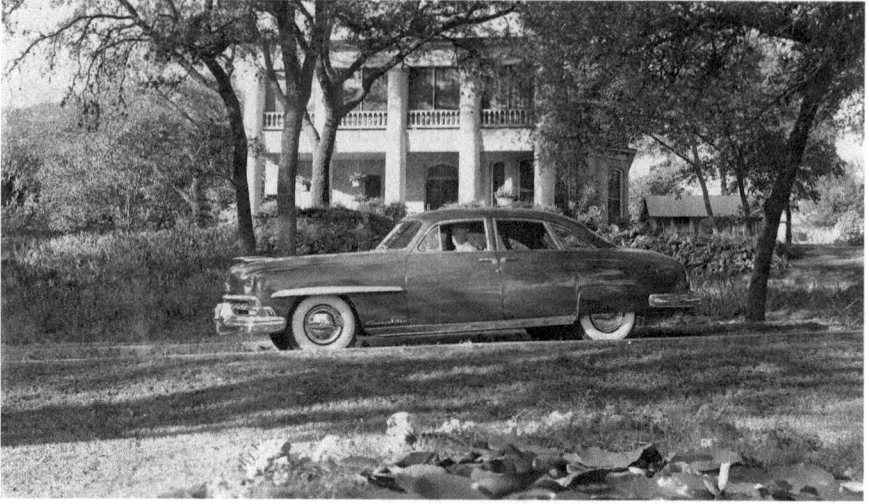

Lawrence Kelley Smoot in his new 1950 Lincoln Cosmopolitan on the Flower Hill driveway. *Flower Hill Foundation Collection.*

until midnight to hear the bells and the chimes and the fireworks being shot off downtown. We would ceremoniously turn the calendar to the new year right on the stroke of midnight and we shared some sort of toast. This was very mild, not a hard toast."

"Of course church activities dominated the Easter holiday from the Good Friday service on through to Easter Sunday. After church, all over town, the ladies would go in their best finery, especially in lovely Easter hats, and walk around and around the Capitol building. Many people parked their cars down on the Avenue [Congress Avenue] to watch this. I've always thought that was an interesting combination of the most holy time of the Christian year combined with a sprightly feeling of spring."

A typical Sunday usually meant that the Smoots would go driving out into the hill country after church services and lunch. "We all loved to take Sunday afternoon drives. Daddy knew everything from here to Devil's River like the palm of his hand. An alternative Sunday afternoon entertainment was to go over into Old Enfield and park the car and go through all the houses being newly built. I think I've been in every house in Enfield as it was being constructed. Until the contractor locked the house, it was perfectly alright for anybody to go through and look at it. We would park the car and walk." Jane also recalled parking the car on the Avenue on Saturday afternoon to "people watch." "You could park all day long if you wanted to, there were no parking meters. We would just sit in the car and watch the people go by on the sidewalk. Some would stop and visit, others would just wave."

These traditions, whether on holidays, Sundays or during an ordinary week, were a series of important rituals to the family. "These were very serious parts of our lives. They may have been ordinary rituals, but they were necessary to the order of our lives. It would be unthinkable not to have them."

Faith was an intrinsic part of everyday life for the Smoot family. Jane recalled that there were always morning and evening family prayers and daily Bible readings, and guests and others who lived at Flower Hill participated. "We would never think of starting or ending the day without this." Printed prayers, particularly those of Saint Francis, framed and set on desks and side tables, expressed the cherished values of the Smoots. Jane's well-worn Bible, still at her bedside, with many notations in the margin is confirmation of her extensive scripture study. This story of lost keys in Jane's 1934 diary is an example of the young girl's familiarity with the power of prayer:

> *Today was the last school-day this year! After school we went after our [Christmas] tree. Mother wasn't feeling well and wouldn't go with us, but wouldn't let us stay home, so we went. We went out on the Bull Creek road where we wouldn't get in trouble for chopping down trees. We climbed over a high barbed-wire fence and then up a rocky hillside. We got the tree and were ready to start back when we discovered that we had lost the car keys. We were frantic! We stumbled back up the hill, praying at every step. We were out there miles from nowhere and we wanted to get back to Mother as soon as we could. We got lost and didn't know where we were. Then, crying dumbly, I turned and found the stump of the tree we had just cut and right by it lay the keys! Nobody can tell me praying doesn't do good!*

In her early twenties, Jane took voice lessons from the choir director at St. David's Episcopal Church, and he invited her to sing in his choir. "For about three or four years, I sang at St. David's and didn't go to my church which, in a way, bothered my parents a little bit. But, this experience allowed me the opportunity to learn the litany and the procedure and service of that church. In years later, when my own church began to gradually to creep out in that direction, it didn't bother me at all."

The name "Miss Jane Smoot" is synonymous with teaching excellence, and many years after she retired, former students still recalled the positive experience of being in her classroom. The following story told by Miss

Smoot in an oral history interview perfectly illustrates her commitment and dedication to her students:

> *Early in my teaching career, I had a class of ninth-graders who were as sweet as they could be, but kind of pitiful because they weren't strong students. They didn't have a solid background to prepare them for the study of Shakespeare and their reading skills were poor. I kept putting off studying* Julius Caesar *because I thought the subject would be beyond their capabilities. One day, one of these students said to me rather wistfully, "Well, all of my friends in homeroom are studying* Julius Caesar, *and when are we going to do* Julius Caesar?" *I answered that we would get to it pretty soon.*
>
> *I wound up reading the whole thing to them, sometimes only a page at a time, depending on the material. Then I would summarize, sort of retell in familiar language. As we went along, they began to perk up. They still couldn't understand the language independently, but they were beginning to absorb. Before we finally finished that blooming play, we were all enjoying it. I had a different view of* Julius Caesar *from any I had ever had before.... The teacher always learns more than the students do.*

In an interview, when asked what makes a worthwhile teacher, Miss Smoot responded: "In the first place, she has to have a genuine interest in the students, must personally, individually care about those students. And, second, she must thoroughly know the material so that she can talk it straight out of her mind and her heart."

This successful lifelong teacher, who positively influenced so many students, considered reading the basic foundation for an enriched life. "As long as I can remember I have had a devotion to literature. I grew up in books. To me a book is a friend and every book opens to you another way of life. Reading is enrichment and an adventure. I always tried to help students realize this."

A student in Miss Smoot's senior English class at Travis High, class of 1970, LouAnne Sanders, held the teacher in high esteem. The student knew that at the end of each year, Miss Smoot asked her students to sign her annual, the *Travis Roundup*, and LouAnne spent a few weeks mulling over exactly what she wanted to tell Miss Smoot: "Dear Miss Smoot, I have really enjoyed Senior English. I am so glad I transferred from Crockett, because I would not have learned half as much as I did. Your class was always interesting and I was always amazed by your vast knowledge of literature. I

Miss Jane Smoot's English
VIII Composition Class,
Travis High School, 1963.
Flower Hill Foundation Collection.

only hope that I will be as successful as you and that I will enjoy life as much as you do. Sincerely, LouAnne Sanders."

Other inscriptions from students expressed the profound influence of Miss Smoot:

> *Dear Miss Smoot, You will never know how much you have influenced my life. This last semester I feel that I have learned much more than titles and authors. I know I have been taught a lot about the philosophy of life. Forever grateful, your student.*

> *Miss Smoot, I can truthfully say that I have never experienced a class in which I both learned and enjoyed it immensely, until I signed up for Senior English. It is true that these brilliant authors have recorded novel ideas, but they mean so much more to me when you express these ideas. You have inspired me to live a full and good life, as no minister or mother could.*

Senior English student Margy Ross wrote that she was confident Miss Smoot's "vibrant personality" would continue to be "loved by all of your students—past, present, and future."

Gary Alan Thomas, one of Miss Smoot's students in 1964–65, recently visited Flower Hill and shared his admiration for his English composition teacher. "Miss Smoot was gentle but had expectations and held her students accountable. She instilled self-confidence and prepared us for future challenges." Gary explained that Miss Smoot started each class with a quotation written on the board. "We had fifteen minutes to write an essay about that quote, every day. This exercise taught us to focus and quickly organize our thoughts. It also taught me not to be afraid of writing. I had no problem writing the SAT essay and I got an 'A' in Advanced Placement Freshman English at UT. I credit Miss Smoot for that."

Miss Smoot's students may have been surprised to learn of her friendship with famous singer and movie actress Jeanette MacDonald. During the 1930s and 1940s, MacDonald starred in thirty films and performed concerts across the United States.

Studio portrait of Jane Smoot, 1962. *Flower Hill Foundation Collection.*

After MacDonald responded to a note from Jane in which the Austin teacher expressed her admiration for the celebrity's work, the two women began a correspondence that lasted for several years. Jane and her father attended several of Jeannette MacDonald's concerts and enjoyed backstage access. MacDonald gifted Jane with one of the many decorative hand fans from her collection. The unique gift is framed and hanging at Flower Hill. Miss Smoot also owned an extensive collection of autographed pictures of the movie star and other memorabilia, a portion of which is held at the Harry Ransom Center in Austin.

Miss Smoot endeavored to preserve the spirit and as many physical characteristics as possible of the historic Smoot family home. During the 1950s, she replaced drapes, wallpaper and window coverings and installed carpet in some areas. Jane was meticulous in choosing wallpaper that closely resembled the original wall covering chosen by her grandmother when the house was built in 1877. Through the years, Jane had original pieces of furniture repaired rather than replaced with new items.

Jane explained the difficulty of keeping the house clean with unpaved Pressler Street along the east boundary of Flower Hill:

When Daddy sold the lots along our eastern boundary, he gave Pressler Street to the city and for many years it was not paved. The street was mostly just white dirt, and, it seemed that when anyone just looked at it, the dust came billowing out. In the 1950s, I myself carried around a petition to have it paved. I was the one that did all the dusting here in the house. I could have cleaned this house and just let one person go up that street and

Lawrence Smoot, pictured here in 1956, enjoyed photography and woodworking. A number of his woodworking projects are still preserved at Flower Hill. *Flower Hill Foundation Collection.*

instantly here came a cloud of dust. Getting the street paved turned out to be fairly simple. The city required ninety percent of the landowners to request the paving and we owned most of the land, so I was able to get it done.

"The current fireplaces are original to the house—all seven of them," Jane Smoot explained. "However, the mantle [*sic*] pieces are not original. It is interesting how fads control so many things. The house was built with beautiful hand carved wooden mantlepieces and the openings of the fireplaces were much larger than these are now. In the 1890s, it became fashionable to have marble mantles. My folks couldn't afford the expensive marble ones and so they had to make do with imitation marble, if they wanted to be in style. So these mantles are made of iron and at the same time, the fireplaces were converted to coal burners. These still look so good that many people first looking at the mantles think it is marble until they touch it. For safety reasons, fireplace fires were allowed to die down at night, and we used feather beds to stave off the cold. Those feather beds were a threat to me as a child," Jane said. "Feathers fluffed all around me and then put another one on top. I felt I was trapped."

One of the most interesting pieces of original furniture at Flower Hill is a combination—"all-in-one"—bookcase, desk and bed originally used by Sallie's brother, Lawrence. Below four shelves for books, there is an enclosed desk with a folding lid. Pull out the end of the desk, and it becomes a bed with the springs and the mattress folded inside.

Today, the "faux marble" mantel in the parlor is lined with children's banks given to Asher and Lawrence by their father. "When Daddy and Uncle Asher were young, it was fashionable to give children banks to put their pennies and dimes in. The banks in those days were of heavy cast iron. Made to last forever....The one that I think is most fun shows the goat butting the little boy who in turn shoves the coin down the frog's throat. Another bank is a seated banker who accepts a coin in his hand, flips it into his coat pocket and nods his head to say 'thank you.'"

Walking through the house, you still sense the original ambiance of the Smoot home, with some colorful surprises. The downstairs bathroom contains a quilt rack and a towel rack dating back to Richmond and Sallie's home in Kentucky mixed with a large midcentury teal wicker shelf and table purchased by Miss Jane Smoot. Above Julia's bathtub from the Nalle mansion hangs a cowhide and branding iron from the Williams farm in Milam County.

As Austin grew and traffic on Sixth Street increased, in 1975, Miss Smoot felt the estate needed more protection, and she had iron fencing installed around the perimeter of Flower Hill. Weigl Ironworks did this work. Weigl also created a Texas star and installed it above the front door. The work of this Austin company adds another layer of history to Flower Hill. F. Weigl Iron Works was founded by Fortunat Weigl, a German immigrant who had learned the blacksmithing business from his father in their home country. The company's ornamental pieces adorn and protect many significant public buildings in Austin and throughout Texas.

Evidence of Jane's many years of service and her respect for preserving history is found on the list of significant organizations she was affiliated with. These include the Austin Woman's Club, Austin Community Foundation, Austin Humane Society, Austin Heritage Society, Old West Austin Neighborhood Association, National Trust for Historic Preservation, Chancellor's Council of The University of Texas and Austin History Center. She served on the committee for the bicentennial observance in Austin and received the Bicentennial Heritage Award in

1976. She was a member of the First Southern Presbyterian Church (now called Central Presbyterian Church), which her grandfather pastored for twenty-nine years, later joining Westminster Presbyterian Church. In 1977, Jane was honored as one of six "Outstanding Austin Women." She was also honored by Mathews Elementary in 2005 when she was inducted into Mathews Friends for Excellence Hall of Honor, recognizing her ideal example of the school's standard of excellence. In 2011, when she was ninety-two years old, Jane was honored with Texas Senate Resolution 546, recognizing her work as an educator.

The last generation of Smoots, Jane lived forty-five years alone at Flower Hill after her father died. Without Lawrence to help with maintenance, Jane began to depend on those she could hire to take care of minor repairs and maintain the yard. Two decades after her father died, seventy-two-year-old Jane, through friends, learned about John Plyler, who had begun doing yard work for hire. "When I came to Flower Hill to talk with Miss Smoot, I immediately recognized her as a very upright woman," John said. "I knew she had all the integrity in the world and I respected her very

Jane Smoot was an active member of numerous local and national organizations focused on preservation and education. (*Left to right*) Gretchen Alley, Betty Baker, Jane Smoot. *Flower Hill Foundation Collection.*

much. As small and as fragile as she looked, you couldn't judge that book by the cover. She was a strong individual." In 1991, John began working on the grounds of Flower Hill only four hours a week, but as Jane learned she could trust him, John began helping Miss Smoot in the house several days each week, and through the years, his responsibilities increased a great deal. "She was fair, but she was particular about how we handled things. She lived by the Smoot family motto, 'If there is a problem, we're not going around it, we're going right through it.'" After almost twenty years of the working relationship between John Plyler and Miss Smoot, she appointed him trustee of Flower Hill Foundation. John has diligently continued Miss Smoot's desire to preserve her family history and the property. "She was very proud of her family, but I believe she also knew how special this place was and will continue to be. She wanted Flower Hill to be preserved for others," John said. "I don't believe there is anything else like Flower Hill in Austin. Miss Smoot left it as a gift to the city. It was a privilege to work with her."

There must have been lonely times in the large house with so many family memories, but Jane's life was fulfilling, and she continued to travel. "I think I was born with two wandering feet, one from my father and one from my mother, both of whom enjoyed the spirit of going to new places," Jane said in a recorded interview. "Of course, to them travel was on a much more limited basis than what I have enjoyed." Longtime friend Betty (Brush) Ross described Jane as "very gracious" in every situation. "Jane and I have traveled together many times and we belong to several organizations," Mrs. Ross said in an oral history interview in 1997. "Jane was very generous with her home and her time." The two women traveled to Switzerland and spent one New Year's Eve in Vienna. "Traveling with Jane was an adventure. If she does anything, she does it extremely well. During one trip we took a helicopter trip across glaciers alongside the Matterhorn. Another time we flew in a small plane over Mt. McKinley and then took a train all the way across Alaska to Anchorage." No doubt Jane loved these aerial adventures, as she often stated that one of her unfulfilled ambitions was to learn to fly an airplane.

Miss Smoot's many travels were designed not only for her enjoyment but also as a way of sharing her passion for teaching. She used photos and slides from her many trips in the classroom and often hosted theme parties at Flower Hill for friends. "After a trip to Hawaii, she invited friends to Flower Hill and presented us with a wonderful slide presentation of her experience," Betty (Brush) Ross said. "A table was set with native flowers sent in from

(*Left to right*) Lawrence, Julia, and Jane Smoot having dinner at the Emerald Room at the Shamrock Hotel in Houston, Texas while on vacation. *Flower Hill Foundation Collection.*

Hawaii, Jane was wearing a muumuu and she served fruits from Hawaii and mango ice cream. It was a delightful time!"

The love of travel deepened an already strong bond between Jane and her parents. The first summer after Jane began teaching, she, Lawrence and Julia took an extensive road trip to the West Coast, including a stop at the Grand Canyon and Salt Lake City. For many years Jane continued to take advantage of her summers off from teaching and traveled extensively to China, Africa and South America. She often used photos and slides from her trips as teaching aids. Former student Betty Sue (Thomas) Linder, class of 1967, recalled during a recent visit to Flower Hill that Miss Smoot's pictures of the locations of the Shakespearean plays added an impressive layer when the class studied the Bard's work. Now retired, Linder taught school for forty years and counts her experience of having Miss Smoot as a teacher as the motivation that led her to that career. "Miss Smoot was a very empathetic, wonderful person. She was a remarkably effective teacher who always had her radar out for students who might need help."

"There was a depth to Jane that some may have missed," Betty (Brush) Ross said. "She was an accomplished woman, very intelligent and sociable. She treasured her family history. We have every reason to be grateful to her for her commitment to Flower Hill and her contributions to our city."

7

EVER AS EVER

The Smoots and their extended family shared a loyalty and dedication through the years evidenced by many personal notes and letters. A common closing to these missives, including letters from cousins who were fighting in World War II, was the phrase, "Ever as Ever." This intimate message perfectly illustrates the steadfast love and commitment of the Smoot family.

Jane Smoot loved her family, loved her life and loved Flower Hill. She was intentional and diligent in making arrangements to preserve the property and the family legacy, as were her parents before her. Flower Hill, designated a City of Austin Landmark in 1975, is also listed on the National Register of Historic Places and is a Texas Historic Landmark.

In the past 140 years, the home transitioned from a four-room, two-story house into fourteen rooms, four hallways, four porches, seven fireplaces, three bathrooms and a cellar. Various parcels of land were sold and deeded to others through the years, leaving 1.38 acres with outbuildings, including the lumber room, rose arbor, chicken coop, carriage house, barn and animal stables. Walkways on the grounds were created from paving stones from Congress Avenue, and in 1914 curbing was added to the winding carriage driveway that reaches from Sixth Street to the house. Three lily ponds still accent the front expanse of the property.

The home is in many ways a formal setting, yet it embraces visitors with a comfortable warmth. Virtually every piece of furniture carries an interesting provenance and dates back to when Richmond, Sallie, Asher and

Jane Smoot on the Flower Hill driveway posing with her father's new 1950 Lincoln Cosmopolitan. *Flower Hill Foundation Collection.*

Lawrence moved into Flower Hill. For example, the "real" long horns given to Reverend Smoot by a parishioner in 1883 were stored in the cellar for many years. After Aunt Amelia came to Austin, she discovered the horns, scraped them clean with a shard of glass and shined them with furniture wax. They still adorn the wall in the living room.

The large south sleeping porch remains filled wall-to-wall with beds stacked with feather mattresses brought from Kentucky. The adjacent "packing room" was designated as a place to store steamer trunks and traveling valises. Now this compact room with the original pine floor and exposed Butler bricks contains quilts and hat boxes. Hump-back trunks contain Sallie Smoot's keepsakes, and a cedar chest preserves Julia's wedding trousseau.

Miss Smoot organized the Flower Hill Foundation (http://flowerhillfoundation.org) in 2004. Upon her passing, the foundation and trust transferred to her appointed trustee, John Plyler, who continues the preservation of the Smoot legacy and Flower Hill.

During the last few years of Jane's life, the upstairs north sleeping porch was converted into an apartment where she could live comfortably, leaving the remainder of the Smoot home as a house museum. Below the expansive windows in the northeast corner of the room, John Plyler established the "Jane Smoot Garden," outlining her initials in white stone. A birdbath and feeder attracted the many species that inhabit the estate to Miss Smoot's garden.

Above: Willis Maxwell replacing the roof of the carriage house. *Flower Hill Foundation Collection.*

Right: Miss Jane Smoot in the dining room in the 1990s. Flower Hill remained a gathering place for friends and family members throughout Jane's life. *Flower Hill Foundation Collection.*

The last living Smoot, Jane, passed away at home on September 28, 2013. She was ninety-four years old.

Outside the iron fence that surrounds Flower Hill, the essence of this principled family lives on in places familiar to everyone: Central Presbyterian Church (formerly the First Southern Presbyterian Church), the Austin Presbyterian Theological Seminary, the *Austin American-Statesman*, the Texas Capitol, The University of Texas, Travis and Austin High Schools. These institutions and more individuals than we could ever count were influenced by the work and dedication of members of the Smoot family. That positive legacy continues "ever as ever."

Opposite: From the age of nine, Jane Smoot kept a diary, and later in life, she kept dozens of scrapbooks and photo albums documenting her life and travels. *Flower Hill Foundation Collection.*

Appendix
JANE SMOOT DIARIES

1932–35

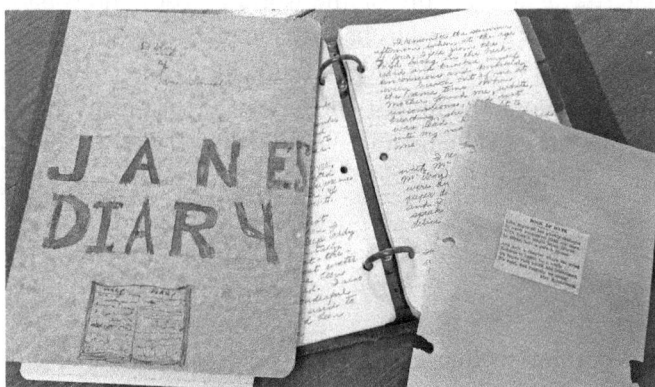

SELECTED ENTRIES

March 2, 1932

The paper said this morning that the Lindbergh baby had been stolen. Mrs. Lindbergh is looking for another one in May. It's so awful for a baby just 20 mo. old to be taken for ransom.

March 3, 1932

Baby still missing; police, detectives, etc. hunting and searching for it. I feel s<u>o</u> sorry for the Lindberghs. It goes to show that rich people aren't always the happiest. I'm glad that we aren't rich even if it would be nice to have nice things.

I was chosen to be hostess for our tea, and I must write it up for the "Nugget." I'm not going to give it to Helen either, because she said that she was mad at me.

March 4, 1932

Had Math test this morning. Mrs. Odom sort of frowned over some of the problems, so I don't know what I made. I was the first to hand in my paper.

Baby still missing. The paper had the prettiest picture of Anne in it. It had the "latest available picture of the world's most famous baby." It had him sitting on a chair playing. His hair was so curly. He has gotten a second demand for the $50,000 that Lindy has ready for them. They said if he told anyone that "that would be his last tale." I guess that means they would kill him. I hope they won't kill him, and that the baby will be safely returned.

We've had a tiff with Helen.

March 5, 1932

We've heard nothing further about the Lindbergh case except that on the radio this afternoon we heard 4 speeches about it. I don't know where the first was from, but the others were from Princeton, Hopewell, and from the general store at the end of Lindy Lane that led up to the house. They said in the paper this morning that Betty Gow, the nurse's sweetheart was into it. He had a date with her Sunday night, Monday night, and was to see her Tuesday night (the night the baby was stolen), but phoned her instead. That was funny. The police took a look at his car which was similar to the one in which the kidnappers used, and found in it a milk bottle. There were no fingerprints on the ladder which was found a little way from the house. Mother thinks that they didn't use the ladder at all, but just put it there for a bluff. I've put in all I can think of, but I've cut it all out of the papers and put it in my scrap-book (which is already as full as a stuffed turkey).

Right after dinner today Daddy and I were playing around in the kitchen while Sister was fooling around doing nothing. Mother had left the room for a minute. Daddy was using the door as a prop, and as I gave him a final tickle the door opened he fell back on Mother. I thought I would have a fit laughing. When I laughed, Mother frowned, so there we were.

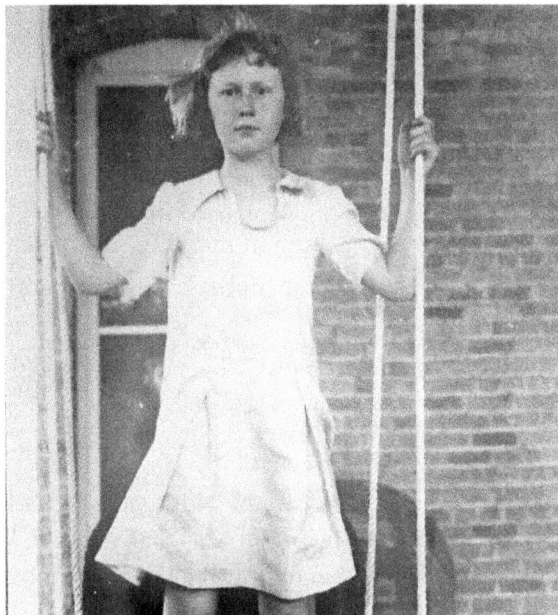

Jane Smoot on the front porch
swing at Flower Hill in 1929.
Flower Hill Foundation Collection.

March 12, 1932

I cleaned up the room this morning. Mother said I did it real nicely, but she changed her mind about it later when she couldn't find anything she wanted. Jule came this morning to wash, but Mother decided it was too cold. Jule churned for Mother and while she was doing it began talking about her "mister" that owned her during the Civil War. Then she asked Mother for a dollar for washing a week earlier so she could get her some groceries.

March 13, 1932

We didn't get up until eight o'clock this morning. That was pretty late. We didn't get to go to Sunday School, but we went to church. Dr. Gribble preached. He preached a real nice sermon, too. Lots better than Dr. Minter.

The cow cut up like nobody's business when we went out to milk her. Mother wasn't feeling good anyway. She stayed out in the cold hall too long talking to Miss Thomas and got cold. Miss Thomas has a warm room to sit in, but Mother didn't. Mother didn't eat much dinner, and no supper. She's gone to bed now and it's not even dark. I'm going to sleep on the porch tonight with daddy.

March 24, 1932

Mother and I went on the street car this afternoon. While I was waiting for mother I suddenly discovered that my purse was missing. In the idle of this catastrophe while I was wondering where I could have lost it, I unconsciously threw the snap on my lunch box, and imagine my embarrassment when all of my leftovers tumbled out right on the side-walk on Congress Avenue! I was so embarrassed, but I picked 'em up and put them back in my box and looked as if nothing had happened.

April 2, 1932

Mother had to go to institute, so I went to the capitol with Daddy. I had to typewrite. I didn't like to, but you don't always get to do what you like. I made mistake after mistake, until Daddy told me to try to not get it perfect, but if I made a mistake to keep on. I acted upon that suggestion, but I made three mistakes. Then, I tried the next exercise on which I made four mistakes. I let them go at that.

Daddy said he wished that I would hurry up and finish my course in typing because he is getting tired of typing 40,000 pages of stuff.

April 3, 1932

Mother woke up sick this morning. She didn't get up, but she had to stay in bed. Sister didn't get up until 10:00 so Daddy and I fixed breakfast, and milked. Daddy didn't get but about one inch and a half of milk. I wanted to laugh, but I knew he was nervous and inexperienced, so I didn't.

During the afternoon Mother got up and we walked around. We had lots of fun. We saw the bride and groom, Billy and Ann, go down the street on their horse.

April 4, 1932

We found out yesterday that Billy and Ann weren't married at all; just visiting each other!

The Wells came over, and brought Willard. They came to the market today; tomorrow they're coming to the florist. That baby is the sweetest thing. He's so fat! Mr. Wells came, too.

April 9, 1932

I had a real good time today. Sister got a letter from Aunt Carrie saying that she is coming up for the Round-up, with a friend of hers. George Jr. is coming along, too. She wanted to ask if mother could let them stay here while they are here. I'm so glad they are coming! Mother's going to write and tell them to come.

May 2, 1932

This morning in advisory Miss Letts handed me a slip of paper that was folded twice, and "Letts" was written on it. At first I thought it was a bad report, but as soon as I opened it I changed my mind. It read:

"To advisor and parents: Jane has done excellent work in 8-A English, and I cannot refrain from expressing my appreciation to both her advisor and her parents. She is painstakingly conscientious, and discriminating.

Jane has also shown a fine spirit of service for the class, which is much appreciated by the entire group.

Cordially yours, (Mrs.) Lois Ervin Pennybacker"

May 15, 1932

We've been quite upset since Thursday afternoon. An extra came out saying that the Lindy baby was found dead on Mount Rose Hill about four miles from the Lindbergh home. It was found by a man who was driving a load of wood…and suddenly stopped the truck, got out, went into the woods, and raised the limb of a small tree under which grew a small leafy bush. He pulled aside the leaves by the bush and uncovered the battered body of poor little Charles Augustus Lindbergh, Jr. The finding was reported and immediately investigated. It had on remnants of a sleeping suit, and a band around the waist. It was all mildewed and in a ruined state. Some of the clothing was taken back to the Lindbergh home. Mrs. Lindbergh was alone to bear the grief. Col. Lindbergh was in a yacht off the coast of Chesapeake Bay. When he heard the news he hurried home to find out if "Are they sure?" He received a sadly grief-stricken nod from Mrs. Lindbergh.

Near the place where the body was found, the police came upon an old burlap sack, a battered spade smeared with blood, and a chipped-up chisel.

We think they killed the child the first night because it cried so, took it off, brought it back and buried it. We think it is very horrible.

June 9, 1932

I have started into summer school good and proper. Yesterday was the first day, but I've already caught on to the hang of things. I'm taking 8B English and Civics. Martha wouldn't listen to me, so she went and took two sciences and a business training. Therefore she has to be there at 8 o'clock in the morning and gets out at 12:00 o'clock. Now what do you think about that? Now me—I go from 10 to 12 o'clock.

Sister has been pulling the cucumbers from her vines and pickling them. They are right good tasting ones but they taste "home-madey."

Mother is taking a course in Education at the University this summer. I wish she wouldn't go but whenever I mention it she answers back and says "Alright. If they put me out of my job then you'll realize what this means. I pull in enough to make a difference in our spending money." That's about so, but I wish she would stay home and nest.

It has been insufferably hot here. We have almost melted. The other day I had to pull a stunt and keel over. When I got reasonably well, Sister brought me "Bluebonnet of the Seven Stars." She's married and has a little boy named Peter. It's so good. Miss Ewing says that most always folks that read a lot nearly always turn out intelligent if not bright writers.

After summer school is over, Miss Green is going to give me and Martha 8A Latin for six weeks, then we'll take the examination from Miss Helen Hill over at Senior High. Anyway, we'll have two holidays during summer school. On the 4th we are going to Galveston and on election day we're going to Corpus Christi. Oh, I'm so glad!

Sister has a job engaged for next fall which may take her to Washington D.C. She said that if she went, she was going to take me along with her, school or no school. That's a grand prospect to look forward.

December 12, 1932

Well, I've gotten my first birthday present. It's been something of a disappointment, but as Mother says, I'll be more aware of its value later.

It is a steel filing cabinet. I imagine it cost like smoke, because they got it at Stecks, and I know Steck asks a lot more for them than Sears Roebuck does, and it asked $24.00 for them. I reckon I ought to be glad that I've got it for I need something to put my notebooks in; I ought to be glad they thought to get such an article that I needed and one that cost so much. Lots of folks wouldn't spend that much. I surely would like to have a horse, though.

January 14, 1933

We've just gotten home from Maysfield; and a pretty lively trip we've had. We left at 9:00 and got there at about 10:30. Mother and Daddy dropped Sister and me at the gate and we had to walk down to the house. It was worlds of fun. We ran into Uncle Hubert at the house and then we went on in and found Aunt Hattie and Harriett. Aunt Hattie had an awful cold, and was in the midst of hog killing. Harriett had me read to her, then we came home. On the way we had a blow-out. And it did blow out! Gave a long piercing shriek. Daddy changed it, then we came on. Daddy has a headache but I hope he'll be alright to go to Sunday School tomorrow.

February 20, 1933

That dog! Honestly I never saw such an animal. Nearly every time you look around she's gotten out. Today she climbed out of that pen just like a monkey climbing out. Walked right up the wire!

My latest vaccination is itching but I don't think it has taken nor is going to.

Miss Farley handed back our outlines today and do you know she gave me C. It made me feel kind of funny. It's been, I don't know how long since I've seen a C on any of my work. I don't mean that to brag. I wish now that I had written one on my life. It could have been real short. As it was I wrote on Irving and it was two pages. Martha got a B and I think considering work and time, mine was better.

June 5, 1933

Oh! but it has been such a long time since I wrote in my diary. Such a wealth of things have happened. Mother is doing very nicely after her operation. Of course, she's had pains and all. Sister went to Galveston and is back. Had review in school, finals, and now all but the shouting, or crying, which ever may be the case, is over, for we don't get our cards until this afternoon.

I've quit curling my hair. It was too hot. We're plaiting it again. Next winter I'll let it curl again.

June 17, 1933

Today is Mother and Daddy's anniversary. Daddy has been worried all week trying to decide on what to give Mother. As its their 15th anniversary he tried to find something crystal but he didn't succeed. So yesterday afternoon he came in with a red, red geranium and three pairs of stockings. She was very pleased.

I'm going to summer school and taking 9B history and Latin. It's just like a nightmare, because Mamma isn't there and I feel so lost without her. The first few days I laid traps galore for Miss Culley. She's precise, and doesn't seem to have a speck of feeling for an individual. I'll have to stand her anyway. Miss Hill is all right. I suppose that's because I've had her before.

November 6, 1933

Sunday was awful because we got up feeling bad, the cow got sick, we didn't go to church. Mother swept the porch <u>on Sunday</u>, and I got help from Miss Thomas's nephew in Chemistry. I certainly think that's enough sins to answer for!

November 8, 1933

We went to Maysfield the other Saturday, and had the best time. I rode Sam's old gray mule, and her name, of <u>all</u> names, was Jane! She was as slow as Christmas, but still she has four legs and was in the <u>shape of a horse.</u>

November 12, 1933

Yesterday we went to Maysfield to take a very fine Mahan pecan tree. We had a grand time. Mr. Gill Newton was still working on the house, and his horse was saddled, so I asked him if I could ride him. He said I could, and when I got on him I began loping him, and Mother began to scream, and called, "Don't let him go so fast! He'll throw you." Well, horsie and I ran all over the Rye Bottom, and I got a blister on my hand. Then Sinator came over on his horse, Dick, and made him say "Hello" by standing perfectly erect and nodding. Fine horse.

November 12, 1934

We had our Armistice Day Program today, and though I never have felt over-patriotic, I must say that I had little shivers all over when the band played and the flag went by. Rev. Allan of the Episcopal Church gave the address, and he got us all so scared…

He said that the next war was not going to be fought in the trenches, but in the small towns and large cities of the U.S. He went on to tell us of the kinds of gases that would be used to destroy whole cities at a time. Gases, some of which, would, when they hit, eat into the clothes of a person and literally burn them up. Some effect the nervous systems of people and when they hit the people they all go crazy and beat and kill each other. Some make people turn green and go into convulsions.

I tell you that man gave me the creeps. On the radio at noon was a program in which Death was personified, and spoke of its power. If I don't have a nightmare tonight, I can't see why.

I don't think I'd mind a nice quiet little war with just a spice of excitement, but deliver me from the sort Allan told of !!!!

November 14, 1934

I got back a weekly paper in Geom. today and got 70 on it. Mother got upset and said it would be mighty easy to drop a second time, so she sent me to Grissom. He went on about I paid too much attention to grades, but I've found that if you <u>know</u> the work and don't get credit for it, nobody pays any attention to you, and now I want grades to get out of Hi School!

November 26, 1934

Last Friday afternoon we went to town. Mother got me a new dress that I didn't want and didn't need. Daddy gave me a pair of shoes that I didn't want and didn't need. They're my birthday presents from Mother and Daddy. The dress is blue jersey—a real light blue and has brass buttons down the front.

November 29, 1934

Thanksgiving Day!
Turkey Day!
Hurrah!

Here at last! I've just finished decorating the table for Mother, while she fixed the turkey. It's raining cats and dogs and is as cold as a dog's nose, so I don't know if we'll go to the game or not—it may clear up.

It did clear up and we decided we would go on as we had intended to the game. But Daddy and I had to go to town for somethings for dinner and for the mail. When we got to the garage, we found that we had a dead battery. Daddy cranked it and we got to a garage before they closed.

Well, the turkey was just too good! We had, of course, dressing and cranberries, English peas, gravy, chocolate cake, and all sorts of fruits and nuts. We just stuffed and stuffed.

The game was a disappointment. It was freezing cold, muddy, and windy. There were the usual ceremonies performed by the band, cowboys, etc. The score was 13-0, Texas.

I think what impressed us the most (and not in a good way) was the vulgarity and misbehavior that we saw. Nearly every other man had a whisky bottle in his hip pocket, and every other woman sucked 2 or 3 packages of cigarets [*sic*] in succession, and both parties vied with each other in outdoing the thing. It'll last me a good while. We were completely disgusted—to say the least!

December 2, 1934

We went to Sunday School this morning, and chose names for our "big sister." You see whosever name we draw is our little sister. All through the year we send them something or other to remind them of S.S. and all. I didn't make such a good draw, but maybe mine will be a good missionary subject. She never comes to Sunday School, and she doesn't belong to the church, and she is a high flier in Society.

January 1, 1935

Just think—a whole year before us with not a smudge on it—just like a clean white page. I feel kind of "uplifted" & yet scared, because I do want to be good and do what's right, but it's so easy to slip!

January 14, 1935

We were proceeding with our usual leisurely Sunday afternoon pleasures of reading & writing and sleeping, when we remembered that the hyacinths at the cemetary [*sic*] must be watered; so we all got in the car and went to the cemetary.

Well, it was nearly dark when we got home, and as we finished backing into the garage & came out, there was Aunt Tucky. It was the same old story—only the climax has been reached. They're going to auction off her prize land—that which has been keeping them alive—in 10 days. Mr. Crimm is soon going to foreclose the mortgage on the Rye Bottom Land & maybe the home. There's been some deviltry played somewhere. Uncle Andrew, according to reports, is still "cutting up" with the scrubs of Waco society, and believe me it's an awful terrible mess if ever there was one. No way Aunt Tucky to support herself (so she says) with 2 girls in high school & 3 boys who are barely able to help themselves much less help others.

Well, Daddy & Sister both gave her $100 apiece. (She just needs $205 to hold it till next year) so we've done the best we can.

Oh, I can't be thankful enough for my dear darling Daddy & Mother!

May 27, 1935

Presents for graduation are certainly coming thick and fast. I've gotten five today, and two Saturday. Miss Thomas came over Saturday and brought a hand painted table scarf and a gaudy yellow necklace. I may be unkind in criticizing the necklace, but it actually was common looking. But the scarf made up for it. It's got the most beautiful colors in it, and when the light strikes it, it shines in places and is dull in others. It has wide fringe all around it. We put it on the mahogany table in the parlor.

We went to town this afternoon to get me some shoes for graduation. They're right pretty, I think. When we got back, Sister informed us that if I was going to get in the University this summer that Mother, Daddy & I would have to go to see Mr. Mathews about it. That I was too young to enter unless on special permission. At first I didn't want to go this summer but now that I find that there's some danger of not going—or not being able to—I want to. I suppose that's always the way.

This morning, having run out of books to read, I searched for something else to do. I decided I'd cut down a white Indian-head domestic dress that was too big for me. Well, sire, no bragging at all, but I got it to a perfect fit. In fact, it's so perfect that if it dares shrink the tiniest bit I'll have to give it away. I cooked dinner today too. And, for a wonder, everything but the cornbread turned out perfectly lovely. But the chickens enjoyed it, so I guess it wasn't really a flat failure.

June 13, 1935

I got a perfectly darling letter from Evelyn Ruth asking me to come to see them as soon as they get moved into their new home.

Well, of course, I thought summer school would be a small matter—that I could just drop. But Oh! No! Mother says once begun, always stung! And that she couldn't do without her "darling child" that long & so far away. Well, I don't feel so "darling" right now, I can tell you!

To see Evelyn Ruth [best friend who moved from Austin to Kentucky] again, to see Kentucky for the first time, the new house and lots of other things would just be too wonderful. And of course it won't be too wonderful, because I can't go at all!! I guess if God had wanted me to go, He'd have let me go. And I guess in the future, I'll do whatever God sees fit, and, of course, it, whatever it will be, will be right."

June 15, 1935

I can't say that excitement <u>never</u> comes, for it has—once! Austin's flooded!!!! Yessir! All the top of the dam is washed off and the water is level with the floor of the Congress Ave. bridge, which is expected to go off anytime, and the Montopolis bridge has already been washed away. The power plant is all under water, so we won't have lights for a week or so! Hot dog!

All of Barton Springs and half of Zilker Park are under water and there are oodles of people here from South Texas, but they're here to stay until the water goes down. The road to San Antonio is 12 ft. under. The water backed up in Shoal and Waller Creek and they've backed out over the streets! All of First, Second, and lower Red River streets are 5 ft. under and it's about a foot here on Sixth St.

Both sides of our front yard are level full and the fish and lilies have floated out of the fish pond and are sailing gaily around the whole front yard!.

June 17, 1935

My greatest ambition is to <u>travel,</u> <u>Travel</u>, <u>**TRAVEL!**</u> Where? Texas, United States, Europe, The World! And I've only been 200 miles from home. What a bitter mockery! Of course, it isn't a tragedy, but I find it awful hard to put fate behind me and smile. Of course, they're always things to be glad of—commonplace things (I don't know, maybe they're best.) But there's nothing adventuresome.

September 5, 1935

Last Monday we went to Galveston, and what a grand time we did have. It was the first time I'd been there since I was a baby, and all the nice things we did! In Galveston we stayed with a Mrs. Aitchison that Sister and Aunt Carrie know. She's the funniest thing! Just talks a blue streak if you'll let her. She has a boarding house and it's just cram full of junk. Some of it is real pretty, and other things are just worthless. Her husband is dead, and then Wop, her old dog died and I think she grieves more for Wop than anybody. She showed us his bathtub and his bed—just like a person's if you please. And then her best friend shot herself and that just about laid Mrs. Aitchison low. She just cried & cried when she told us about it.

September 17, 1935

All freshmen must have physical examinations or will be dropped. Well, I went yesterday to have mine and it seems that all of the girls in the graduating class at high school were there. I knew nearly everybody. I never saw so many naked girls before, and I expect I never will see that many again. They gave us a little apron affair and that was all we could wear.

I've got to take freshman swimming. When I went to get my grade Dr. Crowell said that she couldn't give me a grade and to come see her next week and then she murmured something about my heart and lungs. Well, I know my heart and lungs are alright. I won't mind taking anything but rest. I couldn't stand that very well.

December 9, 1935

Mrs. Tullis came out yesterday for some flowers Sister promised her. She surely is a tight-lipped, stoney-looking person. I know I ought not to talk about her or anybody, but it's a big temptation. The other day I called her Granna Eagle-eye, battle-axe before Sister. It tickled Mother at first, but not Sister. Later when I was teasing her, she hauled off and kicked me hard. I don't think that's nice for a woman of Sister's age to do. It made me mad, and I'm no hypocrite, so I just can't act sweet and loving when I'm not feeling that way. Therefore, Mother said I'd have to be nice to Sister. And, I've got to quit using slang, too. I think I'm improving some on the other.

Mother made herself the prettiest blouse out of an old skirt. It's green, black, and white. It'll go real well with her grey skirt.

It surely is almost like spring. The pears on the pear tree are almost ripe and the trees are beginning to put out.

Sunday, December 15, 1935

I am sixteen years old! Yessir—my birthday was Friday, 13th, so I'm sixteen years and two days old. Mother and Daddy gave me my rust-colored jacket and "Laddie" and, Mother said I can wear her sapphire lovalier (sp?). It's such a beautiful thing that I kind of hate to wear it. Evelyn Ruth sent me a scarf—black and green and ringed around the edges. Aunt Hattie sent me a yellow scarf with all colors in stripes across it. Sister gave me a bookcase, but it's oak and doesn't match my furniture and my room's too full anyway, so we put it in another room. Miss Thomas brought me a comb, brush, and mirror set for my dresser. Mother took the mirror, Daddy the brush and Fluff the comb. Martha brought me a little gold-colored box affair for jewels.

My birthday dinner was beautiful and delicious. Mother is an expert at that! The cake was perfect—pink candy roses and green candy leaves and vines.

BIBLIOGRAPHY

McLeod, D.D., William A. *Story of the First Southern Presbyterian Church Austin, Texas.* Published by the Committee on Commemoration of the First Hundred Years of the First Southern Presbyterian Church of Austin. 1939.

Smoot, Jane. Oral History tapes recorded in 1993, 1997. Flower Hill Foundation Collection.

———. Personal diaries, 1931–1935. Flower Hill Foundation Collection.

Smoot, Lawrence Kelley. Personal essays. Flower Hill Foundation Collection.

Texas State Historical Society Handbook of Texas. Various entries.

Volz, John. *Additional History of the Family and Home Compiled from the Maintenance Plan from 1980.* 2018. Flower Hill Foundation Collection.

INDEX

ABOUT THE AUTHOR

*R*osa Walston Latimer, who lives in Austin, Texas, is the award-winning author of a series of books about the establishment of Harvey Houses along the Santa Fe Railroad: *Harvey Houses of Texas, Harvey Houses of New Mexico, Harvey Houses of Arizona* and *Harvey Houses of Kansas*, which received a Kansas Notable Book Award in 2016. She is also the author of *Spirit of Mercy on the West Texas Wind*, the history of Our Lady of Mercy boarding school and convent in Martin County, Texas, scheduled to release in 2021. Rosa is the 2020–21 Artist-in-Residence for the Flower Hill Foundation in Austin.

In addition to her writing career, Rosa is a writing coach and instructor. She regularly contributes to a national magazine, has edited both print and online newspapers and was supervising director for a nationally syndicated children's television program. Rosa has taught memoir and nonfiction writing at the West Texas Writers' Academy at West Texas A&M in Canyon, Texas, and for the Story Circle Network and offers online workshops on how to write a family history.

Visit us at
www.historypress.com

www.ingramcontent.com/pod-product-compliance
Lightning Source LLC
Chambersburg PA
CBHW070924150426
42812CB00049B/1483

* 9 7 8 1 5 4 0 2 5 0 0 8 7 *